30.6.72

THE GEOGRAPHY OF
RECREATION AND LEISURE

Geography

Editor
PROFESSOR W. G. EAST
*Professor Emeritus of Geography
in the University of London*

THE GEOGRAPHY OF
RECREATION AND LEISURE

Isobel Cosgrove
Demonstrator in Geography in the
School of Geography, Oxford University

&

Richard Jackson
Lecturer in Geography
Makerere University, Kampala, Uganda

HUTCHINSON UNIVERSITY LIBRARY
LONDON

HUTCHINSON & CO (*Publishers*) LTD
3 Fitzroy Square, London W1

London Melbourne Sydney Auckland
Wellington Johannesburg Cape Town
and agencies throughout the world

First published 1972

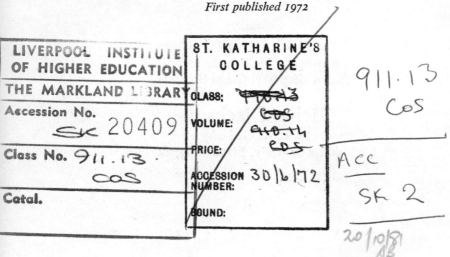
This book has been set in Times type, printed in Great Britain
on smooth wove paper by Anchor Press, and
bound by Wm. Brendon, both of Tiptree, Essex

ISBN 0 09 110260 X (cased)
ISBN 0 09 110261 8 (paper)

CONTENTS

ACKNOWLEDGMENTS

Our interests in the subject of this book were aroused by Professor E. W. Gilbert, Professor J. W. House and Neil Duncan; Professor Bryan Langlands has been most considerate during the writing of this book; Margaret Tinkler read and criticised parts of the draft; J. Mukasa mastered the intricacies of strange place-names during the typing of the manuscript; we would like to thank these people in particular amongst the many who have offered their advice and help. The Geographical Endowment Fund, Oxford, gave financial aid towards research done for Chapter 4.

We have permission from Professor J. W. House, Department of Geography, University of Newcastle upon Tyne; the Department of Arts and Recreation for the Teesside County Borough, and from the City of Toronto Planning Board to reproduce maps. Also from Studio Vista to quote from *Recreations* by J. A. R. Pimlott; University of Adelaide, The Griffin Press from *Mass Entertainment: The Origins of a Modern Industry* by Asa Briggs, 1960; Indiana University Press, Bloomington, from the essay by G. Candilis in *Environment and Policy*, edited by W. Eward, 1967. Any errors in the text are, of course, directly attributable to the interference of Denis and Anne and our thanks are due to April Davies for helping us to avoid most such errors.

I.M.C.
R.T.J.

INTRODUCTION:

THE IDEOLOGY OF LEISURE

The Greek ideal of *schole*, meaning leisure or contemplation, was enjoyed by an élite, while the work of the majority was defined only in terms of the minority ideal, and as a means to that end for society as a whole. The semantics of *ascholia* (work) show a dialectic philosophy; work being the means to the end, leisure, for the Greek nation. For the slaves, however, *ascholia* was an end in itself. But even at that time the citizens could see a stage when a large proportion of the population would have time free from the necessity to work. Aristotle predicted that 'the only one condition in which we can imagine managers not needing subordinates . . . would be that each instrument could do its own work, at the word of command or by intelligent anticipation like the Statues of Daedalus . . .'.[1] This must be one of his more accurate statements about the future. In every society there has always been what could be described as a leisured élite. By definition, this group was dependent on the work of others for their survival; they could be called the parasites in society.

After the Reformation the misunderstood Puritan aftermath of the Lutheran and Calvinistic doctrines was based on an ethic of salvation through hard work. This became one of the fundamental and most revered values of the Protestant world, and eventually of newly emergent Capitalist society.* It could, therefore, be said that the religion of Protestantism was at least indirectly responsible for the

[1] Superior figures refer to end-of-chapter notes.
* For a more detailed analysis of the relationship between religious belief and attitudes to work and leisure see *Future of Work and Leisure* by Dr S. Parker, McGibbon and Kee, 1971 (ch. 3 in particular).

very radically changed attitudes of its adherents towards work and leisure. Instead of work being a means of gaining time and money for leisure, it became a means to eternal salvation, and as such within the confines of human existence and experience, an end itself. Work was good. To be active and productive was to be seen to be working, and so to be seen to be aiming towards eternal life. Leisure was, therefore, superfluous, unnecessary, even bad, unless it could be seen as the means whereby one eventually became more productive; this kind of recreation was the new, acceptable form of leisure paternalistically offered to the Victorian worker.

Max Weber saw the Protestant world as being caught in an 'iron cage'[2] in which the accepted values were asceticism, restraint, productivity, harder work for higher profits, etc. In this cage the Capitalist lost the ability to feel free from the necessity to work, and consequently lost the ability to be 'at leisure', in the classical sense. In fact, the meaning of the word leisure was changed. The early period of industrialisation in the United States exemplifies this change, when society's achievements were firmly based on the ethic of salvation through work. The White Anglo-Saxon Protestant (WASP) moved to a position of greater power and affluence by way of this Protestant ideal, and in doing so lost the art of the Greeks and others—*schole*. An American, Thorstein Veblen,[3] showed how an industrial élite emerged in his society at the end of the nineteenth century. They earned their leisure not through the accumulation of land, as in the Middle Ages, nor through war and colonisation, as in Greece and Rome, but through the acceptable Protestant means of asceticism, restraint and hard work. Because of this, their leisure time was surrounded by a new and very different set of ideals and values. Finding themselves caught in the Weberian 'iron cage' in which to be productive was to be respectable and respected, they were faced with the dilemma of spending their time and money earned in an equally acceptable way. They had to reconcile leisure, which is by their definition unproductive, with the need to be seen to be productive. Veblen's 'Leisure Class' achieved a certain degree of resolution by using leisure time to display their worth, wealth, power and status in society.

They indulged in patterns of conspicuous consumption and conspicuous leisure; a way of life immortalised and criticised by Orson Welles in his film *Citizen Kane*. This élite used inactivity to advertise the extent of their forefathers' activity and productivity. Their extravagant and extrovert tastes and patterns of behaviour were not a means of escape from the cage but simply a way of being at leisure and at the same time indicating that they were staying firmly inside it. The relevance of this élite to contemporary society is that their canons of taste have been largely adopted by a new leisured majority: the twentieth-century middle class. Despite a generally lower level of commitment to work, an increased preoccupation with consumption, there is no real evidence available to prove that the present leisured class find abundance any easier to live with than Veblen's élite did seventy years ago. The hedonistic values of the Greeks were based on an entirely different code of ethics from those which underlie the growing search for leisure and pleasure in the late twentieth century.

Although assumptions have been made about contemporary fashion and taste which see leisure as a 'superior good'[4] replacing Victorian distaste for decadence and their disapproval of all that was unproductive, the old values still have power to keep large sections of the population inside Weber's 'iron cage of capitalism' when they could afford to work less and enjoy more free time. There is at present a tendency towards more evening overtime working. Wilensky suggests that manual workers in the Middle Ages worked approximately the same hours as they do now, and the better paid worked less than they do now. Since the length of the working week has been shortened for labourers in manufacturing industry, mining, etc., we must assume that the Industrial Revolution reversed the balance of hours spent at work and at leisure.

It has been suggested that the Capitalist 'religion of work' is being replaced by a new 'religion of leisure'.[5] The situation is much more complex, and certainly it cannot be assumed that such a change would depend on the number of hours in an average working week. Leisure will never be adequately described or understood if it is defined only as a quantitative concept, that is, the length of time spent not working. Unfortunately it has become just that for the recreational planner, who allocates sufficient land, labour and capital for a population whose needs are calculated in terms of number of hours free from work, income levels, and car-ownership patterns. These factors are fundamental to any analysis of provision for leisure, but they do not always include an understanding of the most important, the qualitative aspects of contemporary leisure activities.

Recreation should not be separated from a consideration of the educational and welfare needs of any urban society. Sport is primarily a social and not an athletic activity. The Arts are not an esoteric amusement for the intellectual élite but an integral part of the entire educational experience. The degree to which they are widely accessible is therefore of vital importance. 'It does not make sense to educate a whole generation to enjoy reading, acting, listening to music, painting, playing instruments, sport, etc., while they are at school, and then neglect to provide adequate opportunities and activities for them later.'[6]

1. Aristotle. *The Politics*.
2. Weber, M., 1904. *The Protestant Ethic and the Spirit of Capitalism*, trans. Talcott Parsons. Boston, Mass.
3. Veblen, T., 1899. *The Theory of the Leisure Class*. New Haven, Conn.
4. Wilensky, H. L., 1961. The uneven distribution of leisure. The impact of economic growth on free-time, *Social problems*, 9.
5. Tilgher, A., 1929. *Homo Faber. Storia del concetto di lavoro nella civittà occidentali etc.* Rome.
6. Duncan, N. S., 1970. *The arts in the South. A preliminary report*. Salisbury.

I

GEOGRAPHY, RECREATION AND LEISURE

If people spend as much time at leisure as they do at work, then the study of the distribution of recreational behaviour as an economic activity is as important to the geographer as the study of coal-mining. The latter has been adequately covered by the discipline, but the former has been largely neglected, and particularly so with reference to provision in urban areas. The reasons behind this neglect must to a certain extent be linked with the fundamental and recurrent problem of definition. When is one at leisure? It is doubtful whether it will ever be possible or perhaps necessary to draw a line between work and leisure which would be generally acceptable for even a short period of time. So many activities are part of both work and leisure; reading, writing, dining and driving a car would all be extremely difficult to categorise.

Various attempts have been made to define leisure. The one adopted by the International Study Group on Leisure and Social Sciences states that 'leisure consists of a number of occupations in which the individual may indulge of his own free will—either to rest, to amuse himself, to add to his knowledge and improve his skills disinterestedly and to increase his voluntary participation in the life of the community after discharging his professional, family and social duties'. The inclusion of phrases like 'of his own free will' and 'disinterestedly' are vaguely discomforting, and the difficulties involved in differentiating between social duties and voluntary participation in the life of the community are considerable. This definition, like many others, is not saying more than that we are at leisure when we have time free from the necessity to work, and it may not be possible to be more precise. It should be emphasised, however, that these definitions are likely to be interpreted in different and even conflicting ways.

A recent attempt to solve the problem of definition included the following 'time-budget'[1] which separates work and leisure by the degree to which time has been committed.

	Fully committed ESSENTIAL	Partly committed OPTIONAL HIGHLY COMMITTED	LEISURE
Sleeping	Essential sleep		Relaxing
Personal care and exercise	Health and hygiene		Sport and active play
Eating	Eating		Dining and drinking out
Shopping	Essential shopping	Optional shopping	
Work	Primary work	Overtime and secondary work	
Housework	Essential housework and cooking	House repairs and car maintenance	Do-it-yourself, gardening
Education	Schooling	Further education and homework	
Culture and communication (non-travel)			TV, radio, reading, theatre, hobbies and passive play
Social activities		Child-raising, religion and politics	Talking, parties, etc.
Travel	Travel to work/ school		Walking, driving for pleasure

The classification does little more than illustrate the complexity and variety of choice of activity, and the difficulties involved in trying to categorise them at all. However, it will be sufficient to say in this work that leisure can be described as the state of being free from

Table 1:1

Indices of change in recreation-related factors, Britain, 1950–60
(with projections to 1985. 1960=100)

Year	No. of cars in use	Total population	Length of standard work week	Av. length of annual holiday	Income per head	No. students in full-time education	No. main and additional hols. in UK
1950	40	93	105	—	—	—	73
1955	65	97	102	90	87	75	75
1960	100	100	100	100	100	100	100
1965	165	103	95	110	115	165	106
1970	220	106	90	125	135	195	120
1975	280	110	85	150	160	240	130
1980	330	113	80	180	185	315	140
1985	380	117	75	200	200	395	150

Source: T. L. Burton, 1967. *Outdoor Recreation Enterprises in Problem Rural Areas*. Wye College, London.

the necessity to work, and recreation is that which one does when at leisure. A number of contemporary developments have made more recreational facilities accessible to a much greater section of the working population. We have moved out of the times of a leisured élite and time free from work has become available to a majority.

In Britain, at present, 47 million people live on 58,000 square miles, own seven and a half million cars, take 35 million holidays a year costing over £600 million. There are ten National Parks covering 9 per cent of the country.[2]

It is predicted that in the near future 'the average family will have a £3,000 per annum income, two or three cars, more than one house, a 25-hour working week and vastly more leisure time'.[3] Forecasts like this can be of general use only because 'changes in recent years in the physical and mental demands of work have emphasised the need for challenging and satisfying leisure pursuits. It is these changes rather than an increase in leisure time—the increase has in fact been marginal in the last twenty years—that have made it imperative to assess, as part of the wider aspects of social and physical planning, the country's general provision for leisure.'[4]

One of the difficulties facing those interested in the effects of increasing leisure is the organisation of factual information which is so varied and difficult to measure. It is important that this be done first so that clear lines of approach and analysis can be seen before rash interpretations are made. Organised methodological research has gone some way towards establishing a framework of recreational theory, and attempts have been made to define the major variables which determine patterns of leisure activities.

The Report of the Outdoor Recreation Resources Review Commission,[5] one of the first to be published, includes a causal analysis of demand patterns, concentrating on participation rates and their relationship to socio-economic variables. The Commission concluded that these measurable determinants account for only 30 per cent of the variance in participation levels. It is clear that fashion, taste and changing life-styles of different generations do account for a large part of variation in demand for recreational facilities. A dominant theme must therefore be what has been called the 'recreational desire line', or how people choose to spend their leisure.

Implicit in the assumption made by many researchers in this field, that activity patterns can be predicted from a set of socio-economic variables, is the hypothesis that each person when presented with a range of activities will choose the one which will yield him the greatest benefit. This will be related to costs incurred, which can be summarised as time spent, energy expended and price paid. Given variations in taste, and environmental resources, the factors of accessibility, disposable income and free time do seem to be the determinants of major importance. They are all interdependent; access, for example, affects taste, and environmental resources do partially explain differentials in disposable income. Individually they provide lines of approach, and this chapter will examine the effect they have on spatial patterns of demand and supply in the recreational equation.

TASTES IN LEISURE-TIME ACTIVITIES

Social historians[6] and social economists[7] have very recently concerned themselves with the effect of advertising and mass media on the way we choose to spend our leisure time. Their individual perspectives are valuable in that they help to place contemporary problems in some form of historical and functional context. Recreation has always been an essential part of the study of any society, but it has never been considered as simply another economic activity where the same methods of analysis should apply. It is therefore important to know whether the same theories of location are valid; if the same laws of supply and demand operate; and whether provision for leisure, as an economic process, has the same kind of spatial expression as do other goods and services.

Since the way fashions change affects how land is used for recreation this must be considered, with other variants, in any preliminary discussion of the geography of leisure. The use of locational theories in recreation studies will be considered later. The basic question frustrating the scientific analysis of leisure time and its effects upon society and landscape is, what makes good leisure? It is unfortunate that many experts have ignored or bypassed this question.

Basically the analysis of taste must rest with sociology, aesthetics[8] and history: some fundamental difficulties are summarised here. Obviously there exists at a national level some agreement on what is the most pleasing way to spend disposable time and money, otherwise holiday resorts would not have grown, nor would Soho, national parks and other areas under conservation. At the same time differences in taste and attitude exist between individuals, within societies and from one age group to another. For some, 'Fylingdales Moor without the early warning station was scenery of high quality; when the station was erected, it ceased to be'.[9] For many others the white orbs in question add an air of newer and more gruesome awe to a well-established bleak prospect. This type of argument is of no analytical value but it becomes increasingly vital to examine the causes of such disagreements as these questions become more and more the subject of public debate. How, for instance, are we to interpret this statement, from the Conservative Political Centre: 'We neglect the proper use of leisure at our peril.'[10] Who is to say what proper leisure is? We could obtain a consensus opinion, possibly, but this would rapidly change over time and from place to place. Thus, the summer visitor to Cannes or Nice before 1860 would have been looked upon as not properly leisured: the towns were then basically winter resorts.[11] A nineteenth-century travel agent openly selling tourist holidays the basic ingredients of which were 'sun, sea, sport and sex'[12] would have dealt in improper literature. The history of recreation is also a story of changing tastes in landscape preferences. On an international scale Wibberley observes: 'Many non-British people do not have our own curious obsession with unclothed, scalloped hills. . . .'[13] He is borne out by Olschowy who has remarked: 'A healthy cultivated landscape is inconceivable without an adequate share of forest, which, depending on the climate, should amount to 20–40 per cent.'[14]

Environment, amongst other factors, guides taste: taste guides the use of the environment. This is not, even so, an insoluble conundrum. In the first place, we know something of the mechanism of changes in taste. The impact of technology is continually altering our assessment of what makes good leisure. For example, Bogart, in a study on the effects of the spread of television receivers, showed that this innovation has tended to reduce reading and attendance at cinemas, theatres, and places of historic interest, had increased attendance at art galleries and at spectator sports, and had little effect on participation in gardening, social and political organisations.[15] The causal links in his work are, however, not very clearly defined.

Second, it is generally known that tastes differ between socio-economic groups, income groups, and people of different educational standards. More especially, it is generally agreed that 'the less educated a person is, the more his leisure will depend on his customary environment . . .'.[16]

Third, it can clearly be demonstrated that the class differential in taste has spatial expression. In general, the taste of one group may set standards in one location which another group will try to emulate. Christaller has examined the development of resorts on the Riviera, appropriately using Hagerstand's Monte Carlo innovation diffusion techniques.[17] In doing so, he achieves a strong theoretical foundation for the pattern of development which led to the establishment, in turn, of Nice, Cannes, Juan les Pins, and St Tropez as fashionable resorts. Likewise, Cribier[18] has described the vacuum effect of changing tastes and inclinations of wealthy Parisians and English milords on Le Touquet, a fashionable prewar resort. This vacuum has now been filled by the Amienois bourgeoisie weekenders and holiday cottagers.

Taste, one of the most important interdependent variables influencing leisure activity, is thus not without its own determining factors and it is the variable about which least is known at present. Until more work is done on this subject we should beware of such statements as: 'The single most desirable characteristic of recreational land is the presence of water.'[19] It would seem that there are no eternal truths governing demand for leisure-time facilities. However much we learn about taste mechanisms and their impact, it is clear that this will remain a random variable in recreational studies for some time to come: 'It is an inherent danger in this kind of tentative prediction that changes in taste and fashion will reverse what appears to be the logical trend.'[20] Many would say that such unpredictibility was essential to the very nature of leisure.

THE LEISURE ENVIRONMENT AND ITS RESOURCES

One of the great difficulties facing those who have attempted to establish national parks, to restrict access in nature reserves, or to subsidise the arts, has been the question of economic justification. In Africa, for example, the question can be phrased: why should we, a poor country, waste land on animals to satisfy the demands of Western sentimentalists who have destroyed their own wild life? In Europe, the same question arises in a different way: why should we subsidise the theatre and not football clubs? The problem of placing a value on recreation is raised in political statements like: 'it is no function of government to subsidise one activity and not another' or 'demand will be filled by the market . . .'.[21]

The benefits of recreation, as of education, although evident, can only be subjectively described and not measured. Despite this, many attempts have been made to answer the above questions by quantifying in money or other terms the resources of the leisure environment. Part of the answer, and part of the difficulty in giving an answer, lies in the changing fashions which affect demand. If this aspect could be eliminated, we would be left with the problem: assuming that recreational 'desire' is a constant, what resources are available? In other words, what is the supply side of the equation?

Say, for example, that within the constraints of disposable time and income the sole objects of recreation in France were sea and sun. Then it would be a relatively simple matter to list sunshine hours per year for coastal resorts: Dunkirk 1,597, Brest 1,650, Nice 2,700, etc.[22] The difficulty occurs when one tries to evaluate on comparable terms the presence of sea and sun as separate items. Another relatively simple exercise is the calculation of the amount of recreational land available in any one region, as Wibberley does:

Acres of recreational land per 1,000 population by region in England and Wales[23]			
Wales	150	North	74
West Midlands	150	South East	30
South West	150	East Midlands	20

Given leisure demands, then it seems feasible to compile a resource inventory. The assumption however is rather crippling. How can these hours of sunshine, land acreages, etc., be converted into monetary or at least measurable-on-a-common-basis, terms? How can the planner give priority to recreational land-use when the benefits of such use are not able to be compared with those derived from industrial or residential development? Must he always fall back on 'amenity' as his excuse for such unwarranted priorities?

Burton and Fulcher[24] in a review of the methods of resource benefit measurement have clearly stated the case. Benefits to society can be measured by three components:

(1) Appropriated benefits—the actual payment made by recreationists. This concrete measure covers many forms of urban leisure and commercial forms of recreation in the countryside, stately homes, entrance fees to caves, national parks (other than Britain), etc.

(2) Consumer surplus—that difference accruing to the recreationist or consumer, between what he actually pays for his leisure and what he would be prepared to pay.

(3) Indirect benefit—accrued where there is no charge involved.

Although there is great difficulty in utilising the first component for planning leisure resource priorities, this is a comparatively easy task beside those problems presented by either of the other components: both others are largely matters of taste. More particularly, most land extensive leisure activities fall into these two groups. As Rodgers concludes: 'In the case of most of the coastal countryside and moorland recreation which are so clearly a growth sector, no firm basis for a calculation of [even] carrying capacity exists. . . .'[25] His conclusion agrees with that of Burton and Fulcher[26] and those reached by the National Parks Service of the USA.[27] Most proponents of arts subsidies would also rely heavily on the indirect benefits components. As long as the basis of society is the profit motive, arguments based on non-economic benefits will remain unconvincing to those who have to provide the money.

In the absence of absolute standards for evaluating recreational land resources, planners have turned to relative measures. How otherwise can such ministerial demands as 'define areas of great landscape value'[28] be met? Schemes for the classification of landscapes have recently received renewed publicity. In the days of Burke[29] and Gilpin[30] such schemes could be viewed as innocent amusements at worst, and at best as the theoretical backcloth for the gentry's creation of landscapes which we now consider beautiful. Our latter-day Gilpins, planning officers, willing though they be, are in many ways not so well informed nor are they given such freedom of action as their predecessors. Such schemes for the comparison of relative landscape beauty vary from country to country, and will depend on the scale of the operation.

In Britain several schemes have been proposed. A basic criticism of many is that they rely too heavily on personal judgement[31]. Although in looking at landscape our derived satisfaction is a matter of subjective responses, a more useful approach (for comparative purposes) would refer to quantifiable landscape elements. Clark[32] ranks areas by a points system from 0–50; a maximum of ten points is allotted to each of five factors: uniqueness, number of individual pleasing features, worth the effort expended in reaching the area, comparative beauty, general satisfaction. The last factor seems irrelevant since it should be the sum of the other four. The fourth is redundant since the object of the exercise is precisely comparison of different areas. The third factor is irrelevant in a negative sense since, if the trip was not worth making (by whom?) it would not be made. In a positive sense, however, it does attempt to grapple with the problem of consumer surplus using 'effort expended' in the sense of payment. The second factor is useful. The first is too, provided it states within what geographical limits of experience this uniqueness falls. What is unique to a traveller who has never been outside the British Isles may not be so to a seasoned world traveller. Further there is the semantic difficulty of grading uniqueness; a feature is either unique (10 points) or not (0 points).

Skinner's[33] work is more satisfactory since it depends very little on personal judgement. The factors considered are: access, population, distribution, viewpoints, topography and particular attractions. The first two factors obscure the matter somewhat since these are determinants of how the landscape will be used. In other words, the scheme is one step beyond pure landscape analysis, whereas

Linton's[34] scheme is based on supply features only and is therefore of some use in elucidating Skinner's fourth factor. Finally Coppock[35] has placed more emphasis on water areas, and Fines[36] attempted to establish a world scale of natural beauty by asking a selected group of Sussex residents to rank a collection of photographs in order of preference. Once the world rankings had been established, the same group of people were asked to compare Sussex countryside photographs with the others. Needless to say, Sussex turned out to be a respectably, if not flamboyantly, beautiful county. The more beautiful parts could then be used in designating planning units for the protection of their qualities.

There is some scope, then, for landscape analysis and evaluations and this scope will grow as we know more of the ways in which tastes are moulded. For the moment, we must look on most such analysis with scepticism; the most satisfactory will also be the most flexible and those involving least personal judgement. It will be noted, incidentally, that almost all the works quoted relate to rural or landscape resource evaluation rather than to factors affecting urban recreation.

The priority given to extensive land-use activities in recreational planning has led to a heavy concentration of research into problems of countryside conservation. Hardly anything has been written and little is known about the needs of, and indeed the present pattern of provision for, people who spend more of their leisure time in towns. 'All the evidence points to activity in and around the home, and passive activity in particular, as occupying the bulk of "disposable time".'[37] It is the less affluent section of the urban population, being less mobile, who are confined to cities for much of their leisure. The Victorians provided parks and cheap excursions to the coast. Most local authority planning departments now take an interest in the distribution of open spaces in urban areas. Very few have concerned themselves with the provision of indoor amenities for sport, the arts and other entertainments.

At a conference of the Town and Country Planning Association held in May 1970 a paper was given specifically on the problem of Open Spaces in London.[38] But it is only in the New Towns and a few isolated but enlightened County Boroughs that money and time are spent on capital-intensive amenities such as multi-sports centres, arts centres, and other non-profit-making forms of recreation. The idea that 'it is the duty of a well-organised community to intervene, indirectly at least, in the question of leisure, to ensure that it is not only used for relaxation and entertainment, but also and above all for the development of the personality'[39] is obviously held by a minority. On the other hand, it could be said that the personality is best developed by asking people to find or provide for their own leisure needs. In many ways the inherent problems in this field are the same as those in landscape evaluation.

ACCESSIBILITY

The meaning of the word 'access' is open to wide interpretation, and is certainly not limited to the more familiar use which is that of physical access. Any participation in a recreational activity depends on a knowledge of the existence, location and availability of a facility. It may be accessible in a physical sense but inaccessible in an economic or social sense, as are many golf clubs in Great Britain. Access to Working Men's Clubs is often as closely guarded.

However, to those primarily interested in the spatial aspects of recreational activities there is no doubt that mobility, movement from A to B, must occupy a central position. It may be that the time for the ready delineation of leisure land-use zones is past since the car has replaced the train and bus as the best way of travelling from residence to recreational area, and given greater flexibility to patterns of land-use.

Of the eight major factors determining recreational participation rates in the United States the two most significant were found to be the locations of population and recreation zones, and the access links between them.[40] In a survey of the Lake District, Mansfield showed that variations in physical distance accounted for 85 per cent of variation in trip generation.[41] Hence the geographer's particular interest in recreation.

Today public transport is little used for recreational purposes.[42] Likewise in France cars are increasingly the most important means of access to areas of leisure-time facilities.[43]

Percentage of all French holidaymakers travelling		
	1951	*1961*
Train	60	31
Bus	9	5
Car	24	60

There is evidence to show that in some cases the possession of a car actually reduces outdoor recreation; the car is a holiday substitute.[44] Again, Burton and Wibberley[45] have shown that ownership of a car does not mean that greater ranges of distance are covered; this is of secondary importance. Most of all, the car is a flexible tool which can be used at any time, at personal whim. It is, indeed, 'an extension of the house . . . a room, which can, in effect, be detached . . .'.[46]

Increasing physical accessibility affects all aspects of leisure. For one thing, it reveals latent demand ('demand which is frustrated by such factors as the non-existence of facilities'[47]). In so releasing this previously unexpressed demand, access has had a positive effect on popular taste. It has been demonstrated that car owners in Britain are generally more recreationally active in all pursuits, not just in those for which private transport is essential.[48]

It is now feasible to argue that in Western Europe the state, instead of subsidising regional provision for minority tastes in the arts, such as opera or ballet, should subsidise the transport of touring companies or even of devotees to national arts centres: it is the old problem of work to the workers or workers to the work. Similarly, international tourism is now within the reach of the majority of West Europeans, with rapid reduction in the cost of packaged holidays afforded by air transport.

On the other hand, it is questionable whether social accessibility has increased in a comparable fashion. Whereas Bournemouth or Cromer could prevent ease of physical access in the nineteenth century by refusing to allow the building of railway stations in the towns, such obstacles are now almost impossible to erect. It is a very simple matter, however, to retain land-use facilities for select socioeconomic groups: membership rules are nearly as great a barrier to recreational mobility as the absence of a car.

Basically the motor car has meant the diffusion of recreational activity over wide areas previously untouched by such demands. The holiday resort has been superseded by the holiday region. On the other hand, as noted above, it has also concentrated demand, especially for minor interests, into advantageously located regions, or to those equipped with better facilities. Whilst mobility has, for the culturally oriented tourist in Italy, favoured itineraries which concentrate on 'isolated monuments and small scattered towns rather than on the great art cities',[49] it has also converted Naples into a daytrip excursion from Rome from its previous status as an independent resort.[50] Lastly, increased mobility has emphasised the shift away from the traveller to the tourist: 'Cultural isolation increases in proportion to the speed at which he (the tourist) travels . . .'.[51]

Increased mobility has generated several investigations into the rôle physical accessibility plays in determining recreational demand. At the simplest level, Ritter[52] has suggested that, all other variables being ignored, nearer facilities attract most use. Clawson has shown that 'attendance at a recreational facility is affected by a constant (in-variance) exponential transportation gradient',[53, 54] whilst Cole and Mitchell also show that attendance is a negative function of distance. Comparison of the value of gravity models and systems theory in predicting demand have favoured the latter since this allows variables other than distance or exponential distance, notably intervening opportunity, to be incorporated into the model.[55] More specific work carried out on real situations has claimed to bring other factors to light. Deasy and Griess[56] claim that access distance and intervening opportunity were of 'little or no significance' in explaining facility impact, whereas regional orientation, consumer familiarity and advertising were. The assessments of significances in this work are qualitative and rather suspect as a basis for analysis.

One of the most useful pieces of work on accessibility and trip generation is that of Mansfield.[57] This examined access to the Lake District in cost terms, coming to several conclusions concerning the effects of access improvement. 'If a road improvement resulted in a 10 per cent reduction in travel costs from every zone, there would be an increase in trips from zones seventy miles or more from the National Park.' It is evident from this study that access can be successfully interpreted in cost terms and that despite the pessimism of Deasy and Griess, useful predictions can be made concerning the accessibility variable.

TIME

It is evident that disposable time available for leisure and recreation ought to be increasing. The length of the standard working week has fallen in 'developed' countries regularly, whilst the number of paid holidays has increased. As long ago as 1919 Sweden legislated for a 48-hour working week and in 1965 four-week paid holidays for all were promulgated.[58] In Germany, the number of days of paid holiday seems to have increased from three (1933) to 14 (1945) to 22 (1969) and will rise to 35 (1985) and possibly to over 70 by 2000.[59]

However, leisure without affluence is of little value. We are forced to examine Keynes's assumption: 'the great majority of people would prefer increased income to increased leisure'.[60] Some of the evidence produced by the Pilot National Recreational Survey suggests that the intervening thirty years have seen a change in attitude[61] (assuming Keynes's remark had factual backing). Many men, despite the shorter working week, will work well above the stipulated maximum especially with the incentive of overtime bonuses. One of the difficulties facing investigators has been the marginal valuation of leisure time.[62] If choice patterns between time and income are to be examined it is essential that this problem be taken into account.

Further, the increasing amount of time spent in journeying to
work to some extent counteracts the effects of a shorter work day.
In Britain the time involved in the journey between workplace and
residence throughout the week is reckoned at equivalent to one day's
work;[63] the figure does not appear to vary very greatly between towns
of different sizes.

Wilensky[64] and Pahl[65] in analysing the apparent increase in disposable time have shown that this varies between different occupations. On the whole, skilled white collar workers in the USA are in
fact receiving less leisure time, whilst the lower middle class and the
better-paid echelons of the proletariat are receiving a greater proportion than any other group. If this is so, then the implications are important, since it is also clear that recreational activity varies from
one socio-economic group to another. In this case, we could expect
recreational activities and demands associated with the professions
to increase less rapidly than those associated with the lower middle
class. This assumption could prove incorrect however if the rate of
professional employment or income increased more rapidly than that
of the upper working class (see Chapter 7, p. 140).

The peculiar distinguishing term 'upper working class' is used to
differentiate it from those whom Pahl described as leisured but not
affluent—the chronic unemployed and the old. For these, time is
disposable but non-recreative and not leisurely, because of the absence
of disposable income. Thus the leisured class contains within it not
only those who are in a position to choose between leisure and income
but also those who, perhaps unwillingly, have time on their hands.

A further analysis is required. When we refer to leisure time, when
exactly does this occur? Does it mean an extra hour each day, or
longer weekends, or longer periods of paid holiday, or all of these
things? The range of activity and level of recreational demand clearly
vary according to the form of disposable time available and gained.
Is it, for example, concentrated or dispersed?

On the daily level it has been shown that the reduction of the working week in the USSR from $5\frac{1}{2}$ to 5 days has resulted in 4–5 hours of
extra leisure time 'in the strictest sense of the term',[66] which has been
distributed throughout the week. This distribution has taken place
partly because domestic chores, shopping and household maintenance have been reallocated by the families concerned. It was reported
that only one-third of those workers involved thought that they had
actually gained additional recreational opportunities; which points
once again to the fact that time might be a necessary, but is not a
sufficient, cause for recreational demand.

On the weekly level, there is a clash of opinion as to what is likely to happen. Rodgers believes that the workshift will replace the work-day and that the weekend will become indistinguishable from the week day.[67] The result will be that leisure normally taken at crowded weekends will be spread more evenly throughout the week. This might well be the case for manufacturing industry but it is probably neither a desirable nor a likely development in the professions. An opposite view is taken by Wilensky and Pahl;[68] the discipline and inflexibility of work schedules will increase as will the 'bunching' of leisured time. This would imply that more inter-regional rather than intra-regional travel for leisure will be possible. Bunching of holidays into weeks rather than days is likely to continue.

Increasing time and accessibility to international tourism may mean that the holidays of west Europeans will increasingly be less concentrated into the months of July and August. In Britain there is little evidence of this. During 1951, 64 per cent of all main holidays were taken in these two months; in 1967 the figure was exactly the same. On the other hand, seven million took additional holidays in 1967 and 25 per cent were between October and April.[69]

INCOME

The general relationship between income and recreational activity is readily stated: expenditure on leisure increases more rapidly than income increments, or as Mansfield puts it 'Income elasticity of demand for pleasure is more than one'.[70] More precise statements, however, are rather less simply made, yet such precision is required if the future impact of rising income is to be assessed with any accuracy. It is clear, for example, that there exists a threshold income above which expenditure on recreational activities begins to increase rapidly, but it is unclear what this threshold is. In the field of inter-national tourism it is somewhere in the region of four or five hundred US dollars annual income, if National Income per capita figures can be used as a guide; expenditure per head at 1,000 dollars average income is about 8 to 10 dollars and at 2,000 dollars is 35 to 45 dollars, with major variations due to location and size of individual countries. Yet this is only a very rough guide, since the individual receiving 400 dollars annual income is extremely unlikely to figure as an inter-national tourist. Indices of national equitability of income distribu-tion need to be integrated with these figures, if they are to be of more value.

Similarly, it is essential to know how income is distributed accord-ing to age/marital status groups. It is obvious that the old are the least active, have excess leisure in relation to income and are passively recreative: the young, unmarried person is physically active, has a relatively large disposable income and a reasonably flexible time budget, few family commitments, etc. At a national level, therefore, 'there is no "national" recreational man (or woman) whose use of leisure may be taken as typical . . .'.[71] Neither national figures nor individual budgets are entirely satisfactory for analytical purposes.

Despite these problems, much research has been done on the relationship between recreation and income. The ORRRC used indices of participation rates by socio-economic groups for predicting growth patterns in US outdoor leisure.[72] Other research in Britain[73] has concluded that low income groups have the lowest activity rates, especially during the week and at weekends. They also indulge more in passive rather than active recreational pursuits. High income groups, above £1,500 per annum, show a very different pattern. Significantly their activities exert greater land-use demands even though some may not be intrinsically expensive.

Watching organised sport, participation in bowls and cycling etc. characterise the first group, whereas riding, sailing, camping and hill-walking are more attractive to the second. This is a clear example of participation rates illustrating demand which is satisfied and excluding the latent demand factor. It may be true to say that increasing income in Britain will mean a much more rapid increase in recreational land-use demand. On the other hand, perhaps taste is more important than income, or as Rodgers puts it 'Life-style . . . not income . . . is the essential key.'[74] Cycling is now a low-income activity, but in the 1890s it was the fashion amongst the aristocracy to spend one's time cycling in Battersea Park.

At present in Britain 9 per cent of national personal income is spent on leisure.[75] If, as suggested in Table 1:1, incomes double in real terms by 1985 we should expect leisure expenditure to rise to the region of 20–30 per cent. In Germany Wagenführ[76] has estimated that expenditure on leisure by 1975 will be approximately 25 per cent and by 2000 may have reached 60 per cent of total personal income. However accurate these predictions are, it is certain that demand for recreational facilities and land for leisure will increase at a faster rate than income.

Recreational amenities are thus resources, neither more nor less than Fenland soils or North Sea gas. They can be created and destroyed. Changing technology can reveal new uses for previously undervalued areas of supply. Like all else their exploitation has to be regulated. 'We take our pleasures, as we make our goods, in mutually dependent groups. Where there is no planning even self indulgence perishes in the coils of contradiction. . . .'[77]

1. Maw, R., August 1969. Construction of a leisure model, *Official Architecture and Planning*.
2. Cullingworth, J. B., 1964. Planning for leisure, *Urban Studies, 1*.
3. Staffordshire County Council Planning Office, 1968. *Planning for recreation*.
4. Central Council of Physical Recreation, 1968. *Planning for sport*.
5. Outdoor Recreation Resources Review Commission, 1962. *Outdoor recreation for America*. United States Government Printing Office.
6. Pimlott, J. A. R., 1968. *Recreations*. London.
7. Glasser, R., 1970. *Leisure: penalty or prize*. London.
8. Clark, K., 1956. *Landscape into art*. Harmondsworth.
9. Coppock, J. T., 1965. *The classification of scenery*. Paper for the Ministry of Land and Natural Resources. London.
10. Conservative Political Centre, 1959. *The challenge of leisure*. London.
11. Ginier, J., 1965. *Géographie touristique de la France*. Paris.
12. April 1969. *African Development*, p. 18.
13. Wibberley, G. B., 1966. Recreation and the countryside, *Papers of the Manchester Statistical Society*.
14. Olschowy, E., Landscape planners' contribution to the preservation of natural landscape. Mimeograph in Countryside Commission library.
15. Bogart, L., 1958. *The age of television*. New York.
16. Council of Europe, 1966. *Leisure in our life*.
17. Christaller, W., 1965. *Geographie der fremdenwertkehrs in Europe*. Bochum.
18. Cribier, F., 1965. Les estivants au Touquet, *Annales de Géographie*, LXXIV.
19. David, E. J. L., 1969. The exploding demand for recreational property, *Land Economics*, XLV, p. 206.
20. Rodgers, B., 1969. Leisure and recreation, *Urban Studies*, VI.
21. Conservative Political Centre, 1966. *A better country*. London.
22. Ginier, J. op. cit.
23. Wibberley, G. B., 1968. Pressure on Britain's rural land, *Proceedings of the 22nd Oxford farming conference*.
24. Burton, T. L., and Fulcher, M. N., 1968. Measurement of recreational benefit, *Journal of Economic Studies,* III. (See also Knetsch, J. L., 1963. Outdoor recreation, demands and benefits, *Land Economics*, p. 387; Pearse, P. H., 1968. A new approach to the evaluation of non-priced recreational resources, *Land Economics*, p. 87; Vedenin, Y. A., and Miroschnichenko, N. N., 1970. Evaluation of natural resources for recreational purposes, *Soviet Geography*, p. 198; Helliwell, D. R., 1969. Valuation of wildlife resources, *Regional Studies*, p. 41, and Trice, A. H., and Wood, S. E., 1958. Measurement of recreational benefits, *Land Economics*, p. 195.)
25. Rodgers, B. op. cit.
26. Burton, T. L., and Fulcher, M. N., op. cit.
27. United States National Parks Service, 1957. *The Economics of public recreation*.
28. Ministerial Circular to Scottish Local Authorities, 1963.
29. Burke, E., 1756. *A philosophical inquiry into the origin of our ideas of the sublime and the beautiful*.
30. Gilpin, N., 1786. *A tour of the lakes*.
31. Lowenthal, D., and Prince, H. C., 1965. English landscape tastes, *Geographical Review*, LV, p. 186.
32. Clark, S. B. K., 1968. *Planning Outlook*, no. 4, p. 15.
33. Skinner, D., 1968. *Planning Outlook*, no. 4, p. 37.

34. Linton, D. L., 1968. Assessment of scenery as a natural resource. *Scottish Geographical Magazine*, LXXXIV, p. 219.
35. Coppock, J. T., 1965. op. cit.
36. Fines, K. D., 1968. Landscape evaluation, *Regional studies*, II, p. 41.
37. BBC Audience Research Department, 1965. *The People's Activities*.
38. Thorburn, A., 1970. Leisure and open space. Town and Country Planning Conference, *Whither London?*
39. Council of Europe, 1966. op. cit.
40. Burton, T. L., and Fulcher, M. N. op. cit.
41. Mansfield, N. W., 1969. Recreational trip generation, *Journal of Transport Economics and Policy*, III, p. 152.
42. British Travel Association/University of Keele, 1969. *Pilot National Recreation Study*.
43. Boyer, M., 1963. La Géographie des vacances des Français, *Revue de Géographie Alpine*, p. 485.
44. BTA/Keele. op. cit.
45. Burton, T. L., and Wibberley, G. P., 1965. *Outdoor recreation in the British Countryside*. Wye College, London.
46. Burton, T. L., 1966. A day in the country, *Chartered Surveyor*, XCVIII, p. 485.
47. Burton and Fulcher. op. cit.
48. BTA/Keele. op. cit.
49. Pourris, D., and Beerli, C. E., 1964. *Cultural Travel*. Council of Europe.
50. Macciavello, A., 1968. Vedi Napoli e poi fuori, *Vie d'Italia e del mondo*, p. 870.
51. Pourris, D., and Beerli, C. O. op. cit.
52. Ritter, W., 1966. *Fremdenwertkehr in Europa*. Leida.
53. Ellis, J. B., and Van Doren, S., 1966. A comparative evaluation of gravity and systems theory: models for statewide recreational flows, *Journal of Regional Science*, VI, p. 57.
54. See also Crevo, C. O., 1963. Characteristics of Summer weekend recreation, *Highway research record*, p. 51.
55. Cracknell, B., 1967. Accessibility to the countryside, *Regional studies*, no. 1.
56. Deasy, G. F., and Griess, P. R., 1966. Impact of a tourist facility, *Annals of the Association of American Geographers*, vol. 56, p. 290.
57. Mansfield, N. W., 1969. op. cit.
58. Palme, O., 1966. Leisure in Sweden, *Progress*, p. 113.
59. Wagenführ, H., 1969. Quoted in *Die Welt*, 6 December.
60. Keynes, J. M., 1936. *General Economic Theory*. London.
61. BTA/Keele. op. cit.
62. Lee, N., and Dalvi, M. Q., 1969. Variation in the value of travel time, *Manchester school of economics and social studies*, III, p. 213.
63. BTA/Keele. op. cit.
64. Wilensky, H. L., 1961. The uneven distribution of leisure, *Social problems*.
65. Pahl, R. E., 1968. Unpublished paper read to the South East regional planning conference.
66. Gordon, L., and Levin, R., 1968. Some consequences of the 5-day week, *Voprosy Ekonomiki*, IV.
67. Rodgers, B., 1969. op. cit.
68. Pahl, R. E., 1968. op. cit.
69. BTA, 1969. *Digest of Tourist Statistics*. London.
70. Mansfield, N. W. op. cit.

71. Law, S., 1967. Planning for outdoor recreation, *Journal of the Town Planning Institute*, p. 383.
72. BTA/Keele. op. cit.
73. ibid.
74. Rodgers, B. op. cit.
75. Lane, L., 1968. Paper read to the 12th International conference of Surveyors.
76. Wagenführ, H., 1969. op. cit.
77. *New Statesman*, 2 January 1970.

2

SPA WATERS AND SEA SPRAY

Several excellent surveys of the early development of resorts, inland and coastal, in Britain are at present available[1-3] and the reader is referred to these detailed and often diverting accounts. In this brief chapter, the aim is not to rival these works but to abstract from them what appear to be constantly recurring themes in resort development. It may be that such themes will facilitate our understanding of present, apparently different, problems.

As with present-day problems, so it is possible to dismiss any analysis or generalisation on the subject of spa towns and holiday resorts on the ground that they owed their rise and prosperity to whims of fashion and historical accident. The visits of royalty to these places are often cited as a major factor in their success—of George III to Weymouth in 1784, and to Sidmouth in 1791, of his son to Cheltenham in 1788—making a change from his protracted stays at Brighton from 1783 onwards—and of royal princesses to Worthing in 1799 and to Southend in 1801. Similarly entirely new resorts owed their origins to individual initiative not to general principles— Eastbourne to the Dukes of Devonshire, Torquay to Palk, Bognor to Hotham, St Leonard's to Burton, Bournemouth to Tapps-Gervis, Burton and Granville. Like the last-named resort, older towns grew through the personal influence of individual medical advisers— Scarborough through Wittie, Tunbridge Wells through Madan, the Isle of Wight through Clark, Brighton through Russell.

Whilst towns were being created, fashionably publicised, or medically extolled, fashions and individual enterprise were also changing the general impulses of holiday-taking. It became more fashionable to be seen at the seaside after 1800 than at the spa; and after 1880 it became fashionable to seek out the sun at the various 'metropoles de bronzage'[4] rather than to cultivate pale, consumptive complexions at watering places in England.

If one accepts these statements at their face value, then fashion, individual whim and random chance would seem to 'explain' the whole process of resort development and to provide all those dynamic elements which divert such developments to new pastimes and to new areas. There would seem to be no place for generalisation. Southey's remarks[5] would be as far as analysis could be taken: 'They frequent a coast some seasons in succession like herrings and then desert it for some other with as little apparent motive as the fish have for varying their tracks. It is fashion which influences them, not the beauty of the place, not the desirableness of the accommodation, not the convenience of the shore for their ostensible purpose, bathing. Wherever one of the queen bees of fashion alights, a whole swarm follows her. . . .'

This, however, is not entirely the case. Fashion or whim may establish a resort town anywhere, but its simple creation will not ensure that town's success. Why, for example, did Topsham, Appledore, Instow, Lymington, and Allonby not fulfil their early promise? Individual initiative in resort creation seems to have operated only within the confines of general economic circumscriptions. Fashion does not explain why resorts grew at different rates: 'Fashion has failed in effecting for Weymouth that which it has done for Brighton, principally in consequence of its being double the distance from the metropolis. . . .'[6]

It is certainly true that within accessible areas (the term is used vaguely here) development of resorts often relied on local initiative or a chance visit, especially before the days of the railway system. One commentator was surprised that Hythe, which 'from its peculiar situation might be rendered one of the most beautiful watering places on the coast', was so moribund in 1849, and ascribed this to the lethargy of its inhabitants who were 'satisfied with leaving things as they are whilst the rest of the world is progressing'.[7]

As an underlying impulse for resort development the dictates of fashion are not inscrutable. Why for instance did spa waters go out of fashion, but continued to be drunk by an increasing number of people? Is perhaps the latter responsible for the former? Why did the cultivation of a suntanned complexion appear when it did? The impulse of tourism is not fashion but social distinction; fashion is merely the florid excrescence of a deeper social segregation. The aristocracy deserted Bath not solely for the sake of a new vogue but

B

to escape the growing numbers of the middle classes congregating there. One wonders whether the *volte-face* of fashion from milky to tanned complexions between 1850 and 1900 was not in fact closely connected with the growth of working-class holidays in Britain and the extension of middle-class holidays to the watering places of the Continent. The fashion setters in their search for social segregation, whilst realising the possibility of price structuring to achieve their ends in areas accessible to the bourgeoisie and working classes, also went further and further afield, colonising the Riviera especially, Spain, Italy and Egypt. It is difficult to disport oneself for long in such places, even in winter, without attracting some degree of suntan; hence a suntan becomes a mark of social distinction by default. This argument is given more force by the secular changes in English living conditions: whereas in 1780 the mass of the English population was still rural and browned by the sun, by 1880 industrial England was peopled by a pallid race of factory and office workers. The stigma of work had changed its colours, and the mark of leisured distinction changed its tone.

The development of the English holiday whether in Britain, or later, abroad is a history of social segregation, and its geographical expression is one of a continuing search for peripheral areas, inaccessible to the excluded classes. These peripheral areas are generally remote geographically but can also be created in otherwise accessible areas by price structuring, or by seemingly minor alterations in the accessibility pattern. The first of these artificial methods is fairly obvious—club membership rules, expensive hotels, etc. An example of the second was the refusal of some resorts—Frinton, for example—to permit rail companies to construct termini within their boundaries.

'Fashion' is therefore capable of analysis, and it can be shown to be motivated by social distinction, which is characterised by geographic segregation. Within the confines of such segregated areas individual initiative may then account for variations in development. The geographic mobility of the different social strata results in continuous changes in the location and extent of these segregated areas. The word 'mobility' is used here deliberately rather than accessibility since access alone did not create the resorts of the nineteenth century. Only when incomes were sufficiently high and when free time was readily available could the facilities of access be fully exploited. The period of most rapid growth of working-class resorts was not from 1840 onwards—this was the heyday of the excursion train. Only after 1870 was sufficient time and money available for the factory worker to stay for a week or more by the sea.

THE PATTERN BEFORE 1780

Before 1780 leisure, an aristocratic characteristic, as opposed to recreation which was a feature of the middle and lower classes, was the norm and it was enjoyed at spas, inland for the most part, rather than at sea-bathing places. The participants were aristocrats; their entertainment was expensive and exclusive; they stayed for periods of months rather than days, often in their own houses near the spa.

The pattern of their activity was resource based. Accessibility played a negative role, for it was essential for the success of the aristocratic spa that it should be inaccessible to tradespeople and stockjobbers. Whilst places such as Buxton and Matlock were geographically isolated, Tunbridge Wells, within forty miles of London, achieved this goal by 'furnishing excellent lodgings for persons of condition; but those which can be hired by the middling or lower classes of society are neither numerous nor very agreeable'.[8] Bath fell between these two extremes: the road to London was improved by the town whilst the rules of Nash and his successors controlled social access. Epsom was too accessible in all senses and too popular, 'clutter'd with Company . . . being so neare to London'[9] to remain an aristocratic resort for long.

The major resorts owed much to local initiative since although the supply of leisure resources in the physical sense—the spas themselves —were numerous, the aristocratic clientèle or market was limited. Whilst Bath and Tunbridge Wells reigned supreme, and whilst Scarborough, Buxton, and Harrogate occupied rather lower places in fashionable esteem, many minor spas were left for the despised tradespeople to imitate the manners of high society in rustic seclusion.

THE CHANGE OF PATTERN 1780–1830

From 1780 onwards the major features of the resort towns were the increasing participation of the middle classes, the rise of the coastal resorts and the increasing significance of location in the success of the resorts. Although Cheltenham only began its rise to fame in this period most of the old spas had passed their fashionable peak, even though they continued to grow in size. By 1806, guide books were bemoaning the fact that Scarborough was now a resort of persons of 'inferior quality'[10]—clothmakers and merchants from the West Riding. And in 1811 Bath was little more than 'a sort of great convent . . . peopled by superannuated celibates of both sexes but especially women'.[11] Despite its status as centre of the fashion world from the 1780s, by the 1820s Brighton was 'thought by the stock-jobbers to afford a salubrious air' and consequently they 'skip backwards and forwards on the coaches and actually carry on stockjobbing in Change Alley tho' they reside at Brighton . . .'.[12]

In the face of this unwelcomed invasion the aristocracy could do little at first, for continental travel was impossible until the end of the Napoleonic Wars. It was, however, possible to escape to such places as Burton St Leonards built purposely as a resort for the élite[13] or to Bognor 'a sea-bathing place of the most exclusive character . . . as could only suit the finances of the most opulent . . .'[14] or to Worthing where 'several of the aristocracy made their usual place of summer resort'. By 1820, however, the Continent was reopened and the aristocracy moved thither, 'crowding around the Folkestone and Dover steamboats with that unmistakable "going abroad" look'.[15] Such German spas as Ems, Wiesbaden, Homburg and Nassau became popular.[16] Switzerland became to the English aristocracy what Cumberland and Westmorland were for the middle classes of Lancashire and Yorkshire,[17] whilst the Riviera welcomed back the milords.

The shift to the sea also entailed a movement from centripetal settlement around the spas to a linear form of town especially when sea-bathing became an accepted substitute for immersion in seawater baths. According to Granville, the factors for a successful resort were the presence of flat, sandy shores, a location distant from a river mouth, and cliffs to add to the scenic interest.[18] However, his factors were somewhat biased by his desire to promote the interests of Bournemouth and, as E. W. Gilbert pointed out, most resorts 'do not have one physical feature in common other than being on the coast'.[19] Within the towns hotels and boarding houses proliferated to cater for the new clientele whose pockets did not run to private houses and whose free time forbade a stay of more than a week or two.

Whilst the old resorts of the leisured aristocracy were being invaded by regional, middle-class holiday-makers, the latter were also stimulating the growth of entirely new resorts accessible to the larger cities, especially London. 'The Sussex coast, above all other maritime parts of the kingdom, seems to be the favourite resort of the bathers. Its vicinity to the metropolis may have a considerable influence in this respect. . . . In the process of time, should the present taste continue, it is not improbable but that every paltry village on the Sussex coast which has a convenient beach for bathing will rise to a considerable town. . . .'[20] Margate prospered, being 'conveniently situated in respect of the metropolis for conveyance by water (by the famous hoys) or land' and 'is always enlivened by a more numerous company than any other sea-bathing place'.[21] Southend in 1803 was 'almost a new creation'.[22] In addition, the industrialists of the north were moving to accessible coasts. Blackpool, which had 'hardly existed before 1760',[23] was a middle-class creation and remained their preserve until the 1860s. The town of Southport had its beginnings in a hotel built by Sutton in 1792.[24]

THE RAILWAY AND THE SEASIDE 1830–70

From the 1830s the development of the railway network revolutionised holiday-making activities. But the effects of this revolution were modified by the inability of the working class to take advantage of these new means of transport in the absence of regular holidays and adequate income. The next thirty years was one of excursion trains for the proletariat and the overwhelming predominance of the middle classes amongst the temporary residents of the resorts. Between 1801 and 1851 these resorts were the fastest growing towns in Britain, but most of the increase was accounted for by towns on the south-east coast. As late as 1871 the northern resorts were still relatively small towns—Scarborough had a population of less than 20,000, and Blackpool one of only 6,000.

It should also be remembered that the steamboat had already shown what effect a rapid and cheap means of transport could have upon the style and popularity of a resort. Steamers had already made Margate the first popular resort; in 1830 over 100,000 visitors came by boat from London. At Margate 'visitors, like mackerel, are valued only by the shoal and the amusements are consequently chiefly adapted for the Million'.[25] Steamers, long before the coming of the railway, had conveyed hundreds of thousands of Liverpudlians across the Mersey to New Brighton or even further to Rhyl and Llandudno, and had initiated the Manx holiday industry. Whereas the average rate for coach travel had been 2½–4 old pence per mile, the return fare from Liverpool to Rhyl was 30–48 old pence and that from London to Southend was 36–42 old pence.[26] The introduction of the cross-Channel steamers also allowed the more opulent to escape the masses more speedily to their continental havens.

Nevertheless, the railways had a much more pervasive influence than estuarine steamer services. Entirely new resorts were created by their arrival—Cleethorpes had its origin in 1849 when the main Grimsby line was completed and branch lines in 1871–3 and 1877 created Skegness and Mablethorpe respectively.[27] But, for the most part, the early period was that of the excursion train: 'hardly a day has passed during the past fortnight without a "cheap trip" from some of the towns of Yorkshire and Lancashire' was a comment of

September 1846.[28] Two years previously the Parliamentary Fare of
one old penny per mile had been introduced. In that year Easter
excursions to Brighton carried 15,000 passengers to and from
London. In 1845 it was estimated 'that 150,000 had left [Manchester]
by the railways' over Whitsuntide.[29]

Whilst this development proceeded some existing resorts shunned
the railways and the masses they brought. Bournemouth, for example, ignored the new means of transport and its customers until
the 1870s. Other resorts believed that they would gain in tone what
their rivals lost by weight of numbers: 'situated some 150 miles from
London, Yarmouth now afforded opportunity for the exclusive pre-
judices of the wealthy to operate, since the high fares demanded for
carriage by railway so great a distance made a selection of visitors
which the five shilling fare from London to Brighton failed to do. . . .
Yarmouth appears to be destined to take its place as the future
fashionable watering place of the élite of the aristocracy.'[30] A vain
hope.

THE HEYDAY OF THE RESORTS 1870–1930

From 1870 the holiday resorts became more and more pre-eminently
the playgrounds of the working class. The aristocracy continued to
pass its winters on the continent searching out new and more secluded
retreats. In 1889, Queen Victoria visited Biarritz and for a twenty-
year period this corner of France became the focus of the English
aristocracy. For a time, too, Pau earned a similar reputation and the
various Promenades des Anglais and Rues Eduoard VII flourished
there.

The reason for this continual shifting was the pressure exerted on
the established retreats by a new phenomenon—the middle-class
English tourist abroad. Thomas Cook, after his successful tours to
the Paris Exhibition of 1855, was organising trips all over the Continent, with the help of the newly established railway network. Scorn
was poured upon such tours, yet in essence they were little different
from the aristocratic Grand Tour in the course of which 'the tourist
contrived to cover as much ground as possible on what was often his
only trip to the Continent. Few strayed from the well-trodden
paths.'[31] Whilst approximately 100,000 cross-Channel trips were
made in 1835, there were 500,000 in 1882 and over a million by
1901.[32]

The impetus for continental travel by the middle classes was given
partly by the desire to emulate upper-class fashions, partly by a dis-
interested wish to see the world and partly by the increasing pressure
brought to their previously favourite resorts by the working-class

holidaymaker. The resorts grew in response to the patronage of the latter from a total population of 390,000 in 1851 to 1,155,000 by 1901.[33] The mode of transport was still the railway, which meant that this massive invasion, brought about by better wages and regular holidays, was concentrated at only certain points along the coast. Further, most of the growth points were regional resorts, serving nearby industrial populations—the Ayrshire coast serving central Scotland, the Fylde coast serving north Lancashire and parts of the West Riding, North Wales serving south Lancashire and the Midlands, Gower and the Glamorgan coast serving the South Wales coalfield.

The fact that certain coasts, despite long hours of sunshine, excellent beaches, cliff scenery and interesting surroundings (exactly those characteristics listed by Granville)—for instance most of East Anglia—remained little developed reflects the importance of this regional attachment, even though the origins of such underdevelopment may have lain in poor rail facilities. This factor also helps account for the continued and increasing importance of such middle-class resorts as Torquay and Bournemouth, distant from the industrial areas. However, class segregation was also achieved at such places as St Annes (near Blackpool), Cliftonville (near Margate), Kemp Town (Brighton) and Frinton (near Clacton) through socio-economic measures of inaccessibility. If the popular resorts could attract the masses by the provision of certain types of facilities, these smaller towns could repel them by refusing to provide similar amenities.

Within the popular resorts, the private residence of the visitor had disappeared whilst those of the local people had been pushed back well away from the sea-front, which was occupied almost entirely by boarding houses, a few hotels and a multitude of recreational facilities. The latter were really 'created resources'. As in many other aspects of economic geography, so in leisure and recreation one may see a progression in the location of activity from resource- to market-based development. Thus in addition to private investment in cinemas, piers, theatres, amusement arcades, fairgrounds and the like the local authorities at Blackpool spent nearly three million pounds between 1918 and 1939 on public works such as promenades, swimming pools, parks and gardens.

1939 marks the end of a long period of spectacular growth in the resort towns. From then to the present day a whole new set of coastal activities have been brought into being by means of the motor-car and increased personal incomes. These have enabled the coastline to be utilised more in accordance with its linear resource base than by the point pattern of exploitation associated with the railway-based resorts.

It is clear that however complex the result in 1939 of resort development, the processes which had created it had worked systematically and logically. The motive forces of these processes were those of social distinction. Different classes utilised the changing means of transport to attain such distinctions; the aristocracy in a negative way to escape their 'inferiors', the working classes positively in order to enjoy what free time was available to them. Both the distribution pattern of the resorts and their internal morphology reflect these factors. Thus whilst Christaller's assertion that tourism today is a peripheral activity avoiding central places[34] this is probably true only of the present-day aristocracy or high income groups. Van Boventer's remark fits the historical pattern of resort development in Britain much better: 'It is both a theory of the periphery and a central place theory.'[35]

1. Pimlott, J. A. R., 1947. *The Englishman's Holiday.*
2. Gilbert, E. W., 1965. The Holiday Industry and Seaside Towns in England and Wales, *Festschrift Leopold G. Scheidl zum 60 Geburstag.* Wien.
3. Patmore, J. A., 1968. Spa Towns of England and Wales, *Urbanisation and its Problems* (Eds. Beckinsale, R. P., and Houston, J. M.). Oxford.
4. Ginier, J., 1965. *Géographie Touristique de la France.* An excellent survey of French holiday resorts and regions.
5. Pimlott. op. cit., p. 70.
6. *The Pictorial Times,* 20 June 1846.
7. Anon., 1849. *A Handbook to the Southern Coast of England.*
8. Anon. (Feltham, J.), n.d. 1803(?). *A Guide to all the Watering and Sea-Bathing Places.*
9. Morris, C. (Ed.), 1949. *Journeys of Celia Fiennes.*
10. Beale, C. H. (Ed.), 1891. *Catherine Hutton's Letters.*
11. Quoted in Pimlott. op. cit., p. 100.
12. Cobbett, W., 1823. *Rural Rides.*
13. Anon., 1849. op. cit.
14. ibid.
15. Herbert, Lady, 1867. *Impressions of Spain in 1866.*
16. Lambert, R. S. (Ed.), 1935. *Grand Tour.*
17. Dr Arnold, quoted in Pimlott. op. cit., p. 187.
18. Granville, A. B., 1841. *The Spas of England and Principal Sea-Bathing Places.*
19. Gilbert. op. cit.
20. Feltham. op. cit.
21. ibid.
22. ibid.
23. Gilbert. op. cit.
24. Head, Sir George, 1836. *A Home Tour.*
25. Anon., 1849. op. cit.
26. Pimlott. op. cit.
27. Pearson, R. E., 1968. Railways in Relation to Resort Development in East Lincolnshire, *East Midland Geographer,* IV, pp. 281–95.

28. *The Pictorial Times*, 5 September 1846.
29. Quoted in Pimlott. op. cit., p. 94.
30. *The Pictorial Times*, 12 September 1846.
31. Pimlott. op. cit., p. 72.
32. ibid.
33. Webb, M. J., quoted in Gilbert. op. cit.
34. Christaller, W., 1964. Some Considerations of Tourist Location in Europe, *Papers Regional Science Association*, XII, pp. 95–105.
35. Boventer, E. van, 1967. Land Values and Spatial Structure, *Papers Regional Science Association*, XVIII, 231–42.

3

INTERNATIONAL TOURISM

THE SIGNIFICANCE OF TOURISM

In 1971 150 million people will cross international frontiers as temporary migrants; will spend nearly $20,000,000,000 accounting for about 8 per cent of total world trade; they will be welcomed in almost all countries, socialist or capitalist, of the world as inadvertent financiers of development plans; they will eradicate trade deficits and surpluses; they will assimilate and destroy local cultures; they will cause roads to be constructed and they will re-orient the settlement patterns of whole countries; they will personalise affluence in regions of poverty. The pioneer fringe of international tourism ostentatiously flutters almost throughout the world. And as world prosperity increases, so world tourism will increase even more rapidly.

The social consequences of economic activity almost universally have to be taken into consideration at some stage during the growth of that activity; ideally before this begins, in practice concurrently with its progress, usually when the consequences become unbearable. Because tourism involves the trafficking of people; because it personalises contacts between the rich and poor nations of the world; because a major part of its very existence and success is social intercourse; because it 'is an industry very sensitive to non-economic influences',[1] tourism requires the establishment of a careful balance between economic and social benefits.

The tourist in his search for something different inevitably erodes and destroys that difference, by his very enjoyment of it.[2] The intercourse of cultures can rapidly degenerate into the destruction of the economically weaker one. If Norway, which receives as many

Table 3:1

Tourists and tourist receipts by world regions

	1951		1965		1975 (estimated)	
	Receipts ($ m.)	Numbers arriving (m.)	Receipts ($ m.)	Numbers arriving (m.)	Receipts ($ m.)	Numbers arriving (m.)
Europe	890	16·8	7,270	83·7	19,200	170·0
N. America	668	6·2	2,071	19·4	5,100	45·0
Latin America & Caribbean	392	1·3	1,289	3·9	2,500	10·0
Africa	88	0·5	309	2·1	1,300	9·5
Asia and Australasia	36	0·2	484	2·0	2,000	11·5
Middle East	26	0·2	270	3·4	1,100	15·0
TOTAL	2,100	25·3	11,693	114·5	31,200	261·0

Source: Economic Review of World Tourism, *Travel Research Journal*, 1968. Geneva.

Swedish tourists annually as it possesses inhabitants (nearly four million), is caught between its valuable tourism and its national cultural identity, how much more so is a country like Mexico? In Africa the conflict between nationalism and tourism is particularly sensitive and many African intellectuals are annoyed to think that tourists go 'to Africa . . . [merely] to look at the vast natural zoo and at the primitive peoples'.[3]

It is forecast that 'culture travel', educational trips and active holidays will increase at the expense of purely tourist travel.[4] The success of Israeli kibbutzim in getting people to pay in order to work, for instance, has recently been noted by Albania, which is offering holidays to a limited number of German tourists in exchange for six hours' daily work on collective farms.[5] Both 'cultural' and 'tourist' travel pose social problems. The tourist traveller finds himself in what is to him a familiar spot in a foreign land, and in what is to the native an alien enclave.[6] 'The national bourgeoisie organises centres of rest and relaxation and pleasure resorts to meet the wishes of the Western bourgeoisie . . . the national middle class will have nothing better to do than . . . set up its country as the brothel of Europe'[7] is one extreme view of this problem. But it is a view imbued with truth and echoes earlier, no less forcefully expressed views of Western writers.[8]

'Active' or 'cultural' tourism, though perhaps not as exclusive of clientele or native alike, leads to attacks on a much wider front upon local cultures. In Spain 'with tourism, lax moral standards insinuate themselves, undermining rigid traditionalism and accelerating the process of loss of local roots. Five years ago, foreign women in trousers were strongly looked down on; today the señoritas wear them as if a uniform'.[9] The Greek peasant and his donkey find the springs of Diana choked with motorists filling overheated radiators and families. These are personal confrontations between affluence and poverty; they would seem to be much more potent in highlighting the world's economic disparities than the most vivid essays of impersonal communications media.

INTERNATIONAL AND DOMESTIC TOURISM

The dividing line between international and domestic tourism is made somewhat arbitrary by the vagaries of political history. Thus, ten Swiss tourists travelling 500 km in ten random directions from Berne would register as international tourists nineteen times. Ten Americans travelling the same distance randomly from St Louis would never cross an international frontier.

The international definition of tourists is:

temporary visitors staying at least twenty-four hours in the country visited and the purpose of whose journey can be classified under under one of the following headings:
  (i) leisure (recreation, holiday, health, study, religion and sport)
  (ii) business, family, mission, meeting (*U.N. Conference on International Travel and Tourism*, Rome, 1963).

Despite the work of the International Union of Official Travel Organizations (IUOTO) this definition is not universally accepted and it is still difficult to obtain comparable tourist statistics on a world-wide basis.

Bearing these difficulties in mind, it is important to note first, that international tourism accounts for only 20–25 per cent of world expenditure on tourism. Thus, a total of approximately $60 billion was spent by tourists in 1966, only $13·1 billion of which was spent 'internationally'.[10] Secondly, in most economically developed countries receipts from foreign tourists are merely the jam on domestic bread. In Germany in 1966, for instance, foreign visitors accounted for only 8 per cent of all overnight stays.[11] In Portugal, on the other hand, only 53 per cent of all bed nights in 1966 were accounted for by nationals.[12] Most developing countries have poorly developed domestic tourist industries; jam in the absence of bread has created many economic and social conflicts in such areas.

Table 3:2 shows clearly that tourism of all sorts is closely related to income. But it also suggests that as national incomes grow, especi-

Table 3:2

Estimates of expenditure on domestic and international tourism by country

	Expenditure ($ per capita)		National income per capita ($)
	Domestic	International	
Italy[1]	20·70	4·90	1,020
UK[1]	25·30	15·90	1,560
Holland[1]	27·10	29·30	1,465
India[2]	00·05	00·24	77
Nigeria[2]	00·02	00·20	68
Venezuela[2]	00·80	10·40	761

[1]All figures relate to 1966/7.
[2]All figures relate to 1961.

Sources: Economic Review of World Tourism, *Travel Research Journal*, 1968, 49; *Digest of Tourist Statistics*, British Travel Ass., 1969, 60; *Dev. Digest* (AID) 1967.

ally when they are unequally distributed, expenditure on international tourism at first (under present conditions) greatly exceeds
that on domestic tourism. A few wealthy inhabitants of a poor
country, spending holidays abroad, can readily cause a deficit in the
national tourist budget. Later in the development process, domestic
expenditure increases more rapidly and often exceeds, in total,
foreign expenditure. Later still, foreign holidays again increase in
importance.

TYPES OF TOURISM

As has been seen, the international definition of tourism covers a
wide variety of activities which have altered in popularity and in
time as taste and fashion, as incomes and available time, as occupation and cultural values have changed. Along the French Riviera
winter holidays gave way to summer stays as the early Victorian
stigma of a brown complexion became a mark of distinction and as
railways superseded horse transport. As mobility increased so the
French Channel resorts became *too* accessible to Paris for the taste of
the wealthier classes, who took their custom elsewhere.[13]

At present the major tourist generating regions, north-west
Europe and North America, have relatively little sunshine and historical culture respectively. At present those countries, especially in
the south of Europe, possessing these climatic and historic assets,
supply this vast clientele's needs and constitute the most popular
tourist regions. But this is not to suppose either that former activities
are defunct or that new activities associated with emerging or un-
foreseen clientele will not arise. First, although in England the inland
watering place is moribund, the spas of France languish less,[14] whilst
those of Germany (over 230 of them) still flourish. Although the
mud-baths of Dax are now little used, those of 'Eupatoria' (Black
Sea coast of the Soviet Union) are busier than ever, whilst the
Mongolian Government has recently opened up new mud-bathing
establishments to the west of Ulan Bator.[15] Second, tourist income is
not merely to be derived from sunny, temple-backed, beaches.
Educational tours are international tourism and 'active' holidays
will flourish as sedentary occupations increase. The Japanese Tourist
Board, which believes that 'sightseeing tours are becoming indispens-
able for life', encourages multi-purpose tourism with an emphasis on
industrial and technical tours, and on home visits.[16] Lastly, although
insignificant at present, tourists from warm countries often possess
concepts of climatic refreshment different from those of the north
European. Hill resorts in Indonesia,[17] Cyprus[18] and Argentina[19] at

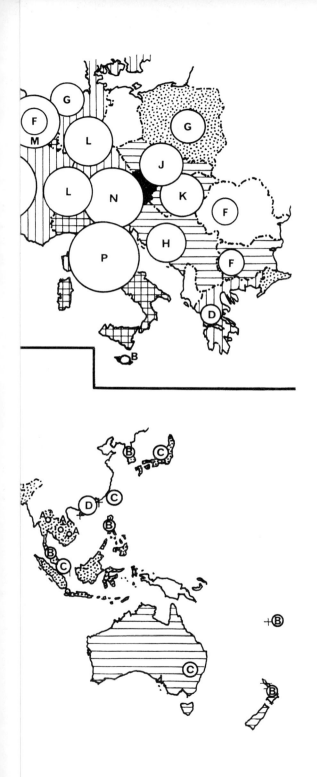

present may be developing only slowly, if at all, but their decline is certainly not inevitable.

THE GROWTH OF TOURIST EXPENDITURE

It would be wrong to suppose that the recent explosion of world tourism is rootless. In 1929 over one million Britons went abroad for their holidays and, in the same year, US tourists abroad were spending $868 million (or 9 per cent of total private spending by US citizens).[20] Tourism was, even then, balancing Canada's international payments and was almost as important a foreign currency earner as wheat.

Table 3:3

Tourism and Canada 1928–31

Average tourist receipts ($ m.)	Balance of trade (inc. tourism) ($ m.)	Average wheat exports ($ m.)	Average paper exports ($ m.)
278·7	+177·2	293·5	136·0

Source: Ogilvie. op. cit.

By 1966 international tourists spent over $13 thousand million, an increase of 450 per cent since 1950, and were spending, on average, 12 per cent more each year. 62 per cent of this expenditure was within Europe.

What are the major factors behind this rapid increase in expenditure? Basically, increasing national income per capita has led to a still greater increase in tourist spending. This bald statement requires both modification and elaboration. Firstly, it assumes a reasonably equitable distribution of incomes throughout the nation in question. Secondly it takes no consideration of geographical accessibility between countries or of the size of such countries. Thus, the threshold at which tourist expenditure begins, and from there increases rapidly, will vary from country to country. Waters[21] suggested a threshold level family income of $10,000 for the USA, although this is evidently much higher than one for any European country. Indeed, the average threshold level for international tourist expenditure for the world seems to lie somewhere between $450 and $750 national income per capita or, say, about $2,500 per family. Thirdly, the rate of increased expenditure above this varying threshold usually increases much more quickly than income increments. The Economist[22] has published a ratio of 1·5–2·0%:1% between the two. This is an average figure;

for individual countries, demand for foreign travel varies partly with incomes, but also with geographical location and other less readily defined factors such as 'propensity to travel', which can be classed as a matter of taste. Thus, whilst the income elasticity coefficient calculated by IUOTO for US tourists is 1·5 (GDP per capita $3,540) and that for Austria is 3·9 ($1,230), those for France and Germany are 3·2 ($1,909) and 1·8 ($1,979) respectively.[23] In general these figures suggest a strong relationship between income and tourism, but the last two suggest that 'matters of taste' can affect important residual trends.

THE DISTRIBUTION OF EXPENDITURE

It is significant that there is a fairly strong logarithmic relationship (r= +0·74) between high levels of national income and high levels of tourist *income* (not merely expenditure).[24] That is, most tourist expenditure is concentrated in those countries which are also the major generators of demand. Notable negative exceptions are the USA (due to its size and remoteness), Japan, Australia and New Zealand (due largely to remoteness). Most of the positive exceptions are micro-states such as Hong Kong, Barbados and Jamaica.

Table 3:4

Major tourist generators 1965

	Total generated		Total intercontinental generated	
	Number (m.)	Percentage of world total	Number (m.)	Percentage of world total
USA	21·7	19	9·8	69
Germany	21·6	19	0·4	3
France	10·0	9	0·5	3
UK	7·5	7	0·9	6
Canada	6·7	6	0·9	6
Netherlands	4·1	4	0·1	1
Belgium/Lu.	3·8	3	0·1	0
Italy	3·1	3	0·2	1
TOTAL	78·5	70	12·9	89
WORLD TOTAL	114·5	100	14·2	100

Source: IUOTO. op. cit.

It can readily be calculated from Table 3:4 that 85 per cent of all international tourism takes place within the continent of origin. In

Europe the close grouping of rich nations of differing climates and cultural histories ensures that most countries both generate and receive tourists. However, it is the poorer countries of Europe, especially of the south, which have benefited most relative to their other sources of income.

Europeans, with the minor exception of the British, tend to travel little outside their own continent. North Americans, however, constitute three-quarters of intercontinental world tourists. Many of these travel to Europe and to small, poor countries, especially to those geographically proximate to the United States, but also beyond to almost all countries of the globe. The share of intercontinental expenditure in total tourist expenditure is increasing as size of demand facilitates the removal of the friction of geographical distance. The American tourist invasion of Europe is only the forerunner of future invasions by Americans and Europeans of Africa, Asia and Latin America.

TOURISM AND DEVELOPMENT

For many poorer countries tourism is becoming an increasingly attractive source of income and a means of financing other development. The recent experience of some European countries in the tourist industry suggests that this *'gisement touristique'* is extremely alluring.

Table 3:5

Tourism and the gross national product 1956–65

	Relative growth 1956–65 (1956=100)		Tourism earnings as % of GNP	
	GNP	Tourism	1956	1965
Portugal	87	696	1·0	4·2
Spain	198	1120	1·3	5·3
Austria	102	383	2·6	6·2
Italy	123	401	1·0	2·3
Greece	116	245	1·2	1·9

Source: R. C. Mings. Tourism's Potential for Economic Development in the Caribbean, *Journal of Geography*, 1969, 173.

Already many small countries are finding tourism to be a more dependable form of income than cash crops. In the former case, competition between developing countries is far less severe because of the rapid growth of demand and because of the generally non-conflicting nature of supply. Whilst coffee is virtually the same product the world over, culture and landscapes are often extremely localised.

Table 3:6

Tourism and other basic sources of income
(1961 = 100)

		1963	1965	Value in 1965 ($ m.)
Morocco	Phosphates	114	142	115
	Citrus fruit	159	162	47
	Tourism	174	264	66
Mexico	Cotton	114	123	212
	Coffee	70	104	73
	Tourism	118	140	782
Thailand	Rice	121	149	207
	Rubber	23	86	96
	Tourism	?	176	25

Source: Economic Review of World Tourism. op. cit.

As a source of badly needed foreign currency tourism is almost without rival in its potential, whilst it is an industry with an extremely high average added value in foreign currency terms (i.e., gross turnover minus expenditure on imports such as personnel wages, furnishings, food, etc.). In Israel the latter figure has been estimated at over 75 per cent of gross turnover.[25] In 1967, then, twenty-six countries obtained more than 10 per cent of the value of their commodity exports from tourism.

Despite these attractions, there are several major problems to be faced. The first is to decide whether the tourist potential is worth exploiting from an economic, social and political standpoint. Secondly, what type of tourism is to be encouraged: mass, low-spending but high gross income (and therefore also high investment) tourism, or small scale, specialised, high consumer cost tourism. Many small countries of the world are beginning to reach this stage of decision. Third, if the former or even the latter is decided for, who is to provide the investment for tourist facilities and infrastructure? —the government out of its scarce foreign exchange, or foreign investors? In the latter case economic benefits to the host country, especially in the short term, will be reduced by the outflow of profits, although local employment and ancillary trades will benefit. In the former case the government must bear the responsibility of the entre-

preneurial risk and is likely to have to forego other cherished
development plans.

For some socialist countries with few resources a short-term compromise of principles may be involved if a situation like that described by Renucci[26] in Corsica is to be avoided: 'capital investments
come from sources exterior to the development projects; they aim at
satisfying demands from outside the island and create profits which,
for the most part, leave the island'. Will, in fact, tourism benefit the
generating country, through profits on investment and through

Table 3:7

Value of tourism compared with that of commodity exports 1967
(Commodity exports value = 100)

Over 100:	Bahamas	250
50–100:	Bermuda	87
	Mexico	84
	Spain	82
	Jordan	59
	Lebanon	57
	Malta	52
25–50:	Barbados	41
	Portugal	39
	French Polynesia	36
	Jamaica	35
	Austria	33
	Fiji / Greece	26
	South Vietnam / Ireland / Kenya	25
10–25:	Tunisia	23
	UAR / Switzerland	20
	Morocco	19
	Italy	16
	Cyprus	15
	Yugoslavia	12
	Canada	11
	Israel	10

Source: Derived from statistics of the *U.N. Yearbook 1968*.

NB: Uruguay and Panama should fall within this list but figures
for 1967 are not available.

foreign travel agents and airlines, more than the host? Certainly the
brokers of travel are located at the customers' end of the tourist line.

COMMUNICATIONS NETWORKS

As in Britain, tourist towns on the Continent grew up in the nineteenth century, at first slowly, as places of aristocratic retreat, and
later, more quickly, as popular resorts accessible by railway. In this
century, especially since the 1920s, the resort has evolved into a
diffused tourist region. Instead of fortuitous development, more and
more frequently such regions are planned, before they exist, around
communication nodes and networks. The development of tourism
in the south of France on opposite sides of the Rhône delta illustrates
this contrast.

By the 1780s the Riviera (east of the Rhône) had been sought out
by the English aristocracy. At Hyères 'there are many houses built for
letting from . . . two to six louis a month'.[27] In Languedoc at this time
(west of the Rhône) the coast was avoided, being malarial, and bathing places were being established inland. In 1868 a railway was constructed east of Marseille along the inland Permian depression; only
in 1890 was the Toulon–St Raphael littoral line built.[28] Resorts grew
along these lines, at first at major termini. Christaller,[29] using
Hagerstrand's propagation wave technique, has shown how from
centres along these railways the innovation of tourism spread to
smaller and more remote centres (from Nice to Cannes, Juan-les-
Pins to St Tropez). This innovation wave, propelled initially by the
railway, has swamped the whole coastal region with the coming of
the motor-car. By 1931, Aldous Huxley could state: 'Forty miles of
Mediterranean coast have been turned into one vast "pleasure
resort" . . . one vast, shuffling suburb—the suburb of all Europe and
the two Americas—punctuated here and there with urban nuclei.'[30]
The Riviera had become the first metropolitan resort region in
Europe.

By contrast, only in 1962 did the French Government determine
to transform the lagoon coast of Languedoc into a comparable, but,
it hoped, better-planned tourist region.[31] Once cleared of mosquitoes,
lagoons were to be set aside for small pleasure craft. A series of all-
inclusive tourist *poles de croissance* were to be constructed within the
region, one of which, La Grande Motte, was completed in 1969.
Irrigation canals and port development on a regional scale are included in the scheme, but the heaviest investment of national funds
is to be directed towards the laying out of a new road network—
about 40 per cent of the total.

On a wider scale, tourism has both been transformed by and helped to transform the world communications map. To a British tourist, a holiday in Japan is only £212 away, the normal air fare being £460.[32] TWA's famous advertisement 'We have shrunk the Atlantic' is no exaggeration. A British tourist can now travel to and from New York more cheaply than to and from Vienna. The social distinctions of nineteenth-century resorts built on the barriers of geographic distance will only be retained in the twentieth-century tourist regions by discriminatory price structures.

An important means of reducing the costs of long-distance travel has been the charter flight and the associated package tour. At present, considerable restrictions are placed by national and international authorities on such flights to safeguard regular services. Thus, selective restrictions of charter flights from Sweden help account for the odd popularity of Gambia, Ceylon, Madeira and the Canary Islands with Swedish tourists.[33] Travel agents usually calculate a load factor of 85–90 per cent for such charters, a figure well above the 50 per cent of regular flights. The result is a great reduction in travel costs.

Table 3:8

Return travel costs from Stockholm

To	Regular IATA Economy flight ($)	IATA lowest* permitted rate ($)	Return charter cost ($)
Mallorca	236	122	65
Tunis	314	151	70
Colombo	854	392	200
Nairobi	782	265	200

* For inclusive tours.

Source: T. Press. op. cit.

Further, because of block booking of hotels, accommodation charges are lowered, and, indeed, it is quite possible to obtain a fortnight's holiday at a foreign resort at a price often only half that of a normal return air flight. It is clear, therefore, that charter flights to developing countries distant from the major generating regions make tourism in such countries quite feasible or at least forseeable.

Distance from the market is fast becoming the least obstacle for would-be tourist regions to surmount. Instead, the problem of massive capital investment becomes more significant. For, if shorter flights bring sources of supply and demand closer, they also mean

that the supplier must invest widely in tourist facilities and infrastructure. Charter flights emphasise, therefore, the size of the leap that
has to be made between a small, consumer-expensive and select
tourism, and a more profitable mass tourism. It is this gap which
makes the decision to develop tourism a difficult one.

LOCATION OF ECONOMIC ACTIVITY

Many countries have found tourism to be especially useful in correct-
ing regional imbalance within their own frontiers. This has been
more true amongst relatively well-developed countries. Here, rural
areas remote from industrial centres have commonly suffered depopulation, relatively poor social services, high living costs, and
deteriorating cultural life. Tourism as a counter to some or all of
these problems has been extremely attractive. In the Hvar group of
islands, Yugoslavia, outward migration plus natural decline had led
to a steady fall of population up to 1950. Since 1955, tourism has
reversed this decline and plans for 7,400 new jobs in tourism will,
if attained, mean an increase in total population of over 75 per cent
to 32,000 by 1980.[34]

In Bulgaria also, tourist development is being promoted to prevent
the stagnation of the Black Sea coast's rural economy and to encourage urban growth. The focus of development here is at Slančev Birag
(on the Côte du Soleil). Hotel capacity had increased from 2,500 beds
in 1959 to over 15,000 by 1968. In order to provide for all-year-round
employment, factory development has proceeded.[35]

Seasonal unemployment constitutes a major encumbrance to resort development even in regions outside north-west Europe. Many
English and French resorts have industrialised for this reason and
most developing tourist regions are beginning to do so. Seasonal industrialisation again adds to shifting economic patterns within the
host country. Even in countries which, climatically, could attract
tourists all year round, marked tourist seasons are created by the
seasonal demand of Europeans and North Americans. Thus, Israel's
tourist boom, whilst shifting the peak month from May (pilgrimages
for Easter) in 1962 to August (European summer holidays) in 1968
has not affected the ratio between high- and low-season tourist numbers, which remains at 2·5:1 (August:February).[36] If all-year-round
employment for the mass tourist trade is to be guaranteed, then it
must depend either on the provision of ancillary employment or
upon a change in tourist habits and the redistribution in time of
demand. For both generating and host countries the latter course
seems much more efficient.

In developed industrial countries the solution to the seasonal unemployment problem is closer to hand. If a modern communications
network can allow a climatically well-endowed region to attract
seasonal tourists, why should it not also attract industry to an amenable location? 'Offer young engineers a job in Denain or Pittsburgh
and you won't see them again; offer them the Loire valley, the sea or
mountains and you'll have applicants by the dozen.'[37] Provincial
France does indeed look to the Loire valley and to Alpine Grenoble
as its models to future prosperity through industrial expansion.
Le cadre attire les cadres.

CHANGING SETTLEMENT PATTERNS

The clustering of permanent and secondary houses around tourist
attractions and along coastlines is a familiar feature on both sides of
the Atlantic. In Corsica, Renucci[38] has described the littoral colonisation by semi-permanent tourists, who have created new zones of
habitation and 'new ways of life which progressively degrade traditional Corsica'. Whilst much of such settlement is generated domesti-
cally the phenomenon of the foreign tourist temporarily domiciled
in his own house in the resort region is becoming increasingly
common.

In some ways this high-cost form of tourism is favoured by the
host government since it alleviates and simplifies the problems of
national investment in the industry. Malta, Languedoc, the Algarve
and southern Spain all supply notable examples of such new settlements deliberately erected by or for foreign residential tourists.
Newspaper articles on such properties advising readers of best buys
are common in West European financial columns. Since such settlements have leisured rather than agricultural communities as their
inhabitants, so their sites, situation, aspect, layout and overall form
must inevitably differ from pre-existing forms. In most ways these
contrasts and their effects are extremely similar to those discussed on
p. 100. The cultural and economic collision of such new international settlements with the old entails even greater problems, but
also benefits, than those generated by permanent domestic 'tourist'
settlements.

SOME EXAMPLES OF TOURISM'S IMPACT
The Alps

In the Alps mass tourism has been a vital industry for over a
century. Many of the region's problems and experiences are instruc-
tive to newly developing areas. The problems have been those of

changing taste in demand, shortening length of stay, seasonality, and cooperation between tourism and traditional industry; they have been tackled with varying degrees of success.

The British were instrumental in bringing tourism to the Alps.[39] Gibbon, a tourist himself according to modern definition, expressed the scorn of the self-appointed select tourist for the vulgar mass: 'The only disagreeable circumstance [at Geneva] . . . is the increase of a race of animals with which this country has long been infested . . . forty thousand English masters and servants.'[40] After Pocock's and Wyndham's visits to Chamonix in 1741 and 1744[41] the Alps had shed their reputation as a hideous obstacle to the traveller destined for Florence and Rome. The early resorts, like Locarno, were centres for summer holiday-makers but by 1865 Davos was receiving its first winter tourists. The town then had a population of 1,680; throughout the 1960s 1·6 to 2 million tourist bed nights were passed there annually.[42]

The British also popularised mountaineering holidays. Ski-ing was introduced from Norway in the 1870s and skating from Holland in the 1880s. The original summer resorts, like. Villard de Lans,[43] attempted first to copy the new winter sports and later to introduce, with more success, forms of tourism such as 'climatism' and health cures which were especially popular amongst German tourists. Wealthy individuals, selecting a secluded village for their resort, bequeathed, as they passed on pressed by the common herd, a legacy of tourist amenity to their favoured valleys. Thus, the development of Mégève owed much to the personal favour of the Rothschild family from 1916 onwards.[44]

The building of roads, trans-Alpine tunnels,[45] rack-and-pinion railways and ski-lifts greatly enhanced the development of Alpine tourism, especially in Switzerland and France. The development of the Austrian and Italian Alps was somewhat retarded by the setbacks to the German and Italian economies respectively delivered by the two wars. Since 1945, however, Switzerland has barely managed to retain its dominance, whilst Austria, both as a centre itself and as a gateway to south-eastern Europe for German travellers, has experienced unprecedented development. The French and Italian Alps have also prospered but rather more through domestic tourism, reflecting the general prosperity of neighbouring industrial regions.[46]

At present, then, there exists an enormous range of tourist activity spread throughout the year, partly a product of the region's adaptation to changing technology and changing fashions and partly a product of its geographic location between the major tourist generating centres of north-west Europe and the host countries of Italy, Greece,

Yugoslavia and Bulgaria. In the latter respect, road transport is essential to tourism's success. Development continues but, as in the past, the favoured localities are restricted in geographical distribution. The 'super resorts' above the snowline in France, like Super-dévoluy[47] or Chamousse, have grown alongside the new-found prosperity and redevelopment of Grenoble, whilst Austrian resorts, previously little known, are receiving those winter migrants jaded by the familiarity of the old-established Swiss ski-runs. Garmisch-Partenkirchen in southern Germany was until 1960 little known by foreigners, although 1·25 million bed nights were passed by German tourists at the resort.[48]

On the other hand, Lugano, in the southern Alps, which had eighteen hotels as early as 1801,[49] now finds through traffic more important than residential. Switzerland, as a whole, has suffered in recent years from a general stagnation in the industry and a decline in the number of summer visitors. It is usually said that Alpine summer tourism suffers greatly from the absences of sunny sea beaches and certainly the down-valley, old-established summer resorts are the weak links in the regional tourist network. Austria, although having overtaken its western neighbour as queen of Alpine tourism,[50] has much greater problems of seasonality.

Table 3:9

Visitors to Switzerland and Austria 1967

	Number Apr.-Sept. (1967) (m.)	Change (1966–7)	Number Oct.-Mar. (1967–8)	Change (1966–7 1967–8)	Total receipts ($m.)	Ratio of high:low month
Switzerland	12·3	−5%	6·6	+13%	575	7·7:1
Austria	34·3	−7%	6·6	+14%	615	44·5:1

Source: IUOTO. op. cit.

At present, it is in the fields of winter sports and in domestic tourism that Alpine tourism flourishes most.

When Ruskin visited the Alps he found that the locals 'spoke with chief fear of the influx of English wealth, gradually connecting all industry with the wants and ways of strangers and inviting all idleness to depend upon their casual help, thus gradually resolving the ancient consistency of the mountain life into the two irregular trades of inn-keepers and mendicants'.[51] More recently, higher-altitude developments have inspired similar fears that those who try to adapt to tourism by establishing small family pensions will be flooded out by large, expensive, 'foreign'-owned hotels.[52] These fears can be justified.

In the Italian Alps, Janin has shown how local hotel ownership is only predominant in the lower valleys, those areas of summer resorts. The newer developments are financed by outside elements. In Davos foreign expropriation of land and property—especially of chalets by German tourists—has inspired cantonal laws limiting such transactions,[53] whilst throughout Austria similar legislation prevents the development of large foreign-owned holdings. In Mégève, even though tourism has not reduced local population or farming numbers, it has replaced local by foreign ways of life.

Table 3:10

Population of Mégève

	Population	Of local origin		Agricultural population	
1911	1,746	1,571	90%	1,164	65%
1962	4,718	2,256	48%	1,179	25%

Source: Veyret. op. cit.

Elsewhere in the Alps, tourism has had even less satisfactory effects on local life. Winter sports especially have been disruptive, since they subvert the traditional employment patterns and take place well above the limit of permanent settlement. The routeways which enable the tourists, the shifting cultivators of leisure, to penetrate such mountain fastnesses at the same time bring in extra-regional produce and encourage emigration of the region's native population. In Breuil-Cervinia[54] emigration continues amongst locals despite overall growth and despite labour shortages. The latter are met by contracting Sardinian or Sicilian immigrants. The number of farmers in the area has fallen rapidly in the last decade, for instead of encouraging local agriculture, tourism has led to the import of milk from Lombardy, butter from the Piedmont and vegetables from as

Table 3:11

Agriculture in Venosc

	Arable land	Sheep	Cattle
1925	300 ha.	546	156
1960	30 ha.	200	85

Source: F. Cribier. op. cit.

far away as Venice. Likewise, the Innsbruck area has lost a third of its farming population since 1951 despite a total population increase.[55] In Venosc in the French Alps agriculture has declined rapidly and the old ways of life have been eradicated rather than transformed.[56]

In the Italian Alps, Bonapace[57] notes 'the contrast between the new uses of the natural environment and the decay of traditional activities that follow montane depopulation—a trend that tourism has halted only in a few regions like Trentino. Below the high permanent settlements of the leisured the old decaying villages of the valley floor.'

In sum, whatever the success, national or regional, of policies aimed at attaining a seasonal balance of tourism, locally this is rarely feasible. In the Alps the short-term local advantages accrued through tourism have been increases in land prices, seasonal winter employment and the development of small guest-houses. But in the long run higher land prices destroy local agriculture, seasonal employment is created for non-local people and large hotels readily displace the family pension.[58] In terms of industrial, economic activity such transformations of the rural environment are common enough. Tourism, however, is no less an industry than steel manufacture and its introduction into Alpine valleys has been no less destructive of total population patterns and traditional culture than if each hotel had been a blast furnace.

Spain and Portugal

Unimportant before 1945, Spain and Portugal are today amongst the most important tourist centres of the world. About 300,000 tourists visited Iberia in 1931,[59] by 1950 there were two million and in 1967, 17·9 million visited Spain and 2·5 million went to Portugal. About 9 per cent of world expenditure in international tourism changed hands in these two countries in 1967, that is, $1,210 million and $258 million were received by Spain and Portugal respectively. Tourism earns about half Spain's foreign currency and over a third of Portugal's.[60] In each country tourism is an invaluable compensation for very unfavourable visible trade balances. Whole regions have been transformed. Benidorm was moribund in 1945; today it has over four million annual visitors in its region. The erstwhile village of Lloret del Mar has today more hotels than Barcelona and almost as many as Madrid. In Spain 'tourism is considered the principal factor in economic development' and rightly so.[61]

Lady Herbert asked: 'What is it that we seek for Englishmen and Englishwomen who, year by year, about the month of November are

seen crowding Folkestone and Dover steamboats with that unmistakable "going abroad" look . . . ?' and answered: 'I think it may be
comprised in one word—sunshine.'[62] Certainly it is sunshine which
attracts the daily summer charter flights from Gatwick, for with this
commodity the Iberian peninsula is surfeited. Places like Estoril,
with over 3,000 hours of yearly sunshine and a mere 100 rain-days,
vaunt their resources.

But who, south of 45°N, is short of sunshine? Iberia's success is
difficult to explain; to attempt explanation on this climatic ground is
patently ridiculous; low prices seem to have been more important.
In the lack of tourist development before 1934, Spain was in some
ways fortunate. Whilst prices in Spain remained low, in Italy and
France high-class tourists demanded high-priced tourism in their
search for social seclusion and had been readily supplied therewith.
Hence, as late as 1962 the relative prices of a stay in three-star hotels
in Spain, Austria, Switzerland, France and Italy were 1:1·46:1·71:
1·75:1·79.[63] The French tourist, during the 1950s, was the pioneer
who first exploited such low prices on the Costa Brava on any scale.

In 1953, at a particularly felicitous moment, the Spanish Government introduced its National Plan for Tourism. Generous loans were
made available to hoteliers, who also had the advantage of low construction and labour costs. Tax concessions were also introduced. At
the same time, charter flights were becoming popular amongst North
Europeans wanting to take their annual holidays at sunnier Black-
pools at hardly any greater expense. The success of Spain indeed lay
in its provision of familiar holidays in an unfamiliar climate and by
mysteriously warm Mediterranean waters. There was little that was
foreign about a Costa Brava holiday except the sun and the cheap
wine, and millions of tourists preferred sunny familiarity; only the
thousands prefer exotic discomfort.

A second phase of Spanish tourism was entered in 1964 when
massive government investment in the industry began. Between 1964
and 1966 over $600 million (about 20 per cent of total tourist
revenue)[64] were spent in spreading the prosperity of tourism to remote
coasts, especially in the south, and to inland towns. State inns (*para-
dors*) were established and more expensive and varied types of tourism encouraged. The result has been the introduction of all grades
of holiday-making in respect of both price ranges and activity.
However, only a small proportion of the low-cost holiday market
potential existing in north-west Europe has, as yet, been realised.
Spain's past use of its fortuitous circumstances will ensure that its
attraction for this market will continue to dominate intra-European
tourism.

Portugal remained a peripheral tourist area until the 1960s. Only belatedly were *pousadas* (state hotels) introduced, whilst government investment in 1966 was a mere $1·5 million. This was despite the fact that in that year tourism earned 25 per cent of Portugal's foreign currency. Since 1968, the Third Development Plan envisages that 9·7 per cent (of about $80 million per year) of all investments for Metropolitan Portugal shall be directed towards tourism. Of this sum, however, 79 per cent will be 'self-financing' and only 4 per cent will come from governmental budget.[65] Priority is being given not to mass tourism but to residential housing developments in the Algarve, where new luxury settlements are being constructed for long-stay tourists—at Faro, Lagos, Montes de Alva and Praia da Rocha.

The case of Iberia suggests strongly that government interest in tourism can be extremely stimulating to the industry but that lack of interest on its part, provided it does not amount to active antipathy, will do little to impede a powerful demand for low-cost holidays. Secondly it suggests that although mass tourism can only be attracted at ultra-competitive prices at a level not foreseeable in, say, African countries, price structuring can effectively control the type of tourist.

Eire

Eire's economic history, a dismal story of colonialism at its worst, has been dominated by ties with Britain. The Dublin region has been, overwhelmingly, the centre of urbanisation, industry and distributive trades. Much of peripheral and mountainous western Ireland, densely populated despite its small area of cultivated land, has experienced continual depopulation since the potato famines of the 1840s. This depopulation has not been coped with nationally, and emigration to Britain and North America resulted in successive Irish censuses (until 1966) recording ever lower population totals. In the attempts to reassert Ireland's national pride, however, the West has played a crucial rôle. For it is to the West that most intellectuals and politicians have looked for an expression of life that is most 'Irish'. The Irish language, compulsorily taught throughout the country, is the vernacular only of the West. Hence, one of the major goals of successive Irish Governments has been the spatial redistribution of economic activity to stem depopulation and emigration, and to safeguard Western ways of life.

Tourism, unlike industry, 'is much more pervasive in its economic impact—it represents an injection of external purchasing power into the economy widely distributed in its initial regional impact and acting as a stimulus to every sector of economy'.[66] In the economic resuscitation of the rural West, tourism has played the leading rôle.

The leisurely English tourists[67] of the eighteenth and nineteenth centuries established the attractions of Ireland for their later compatriots: the lakes and mountains of Cork and Kerry, the wild, cove-studded coasts of Galway and Mayo, the montane peasantry of Donegal, and the innumerable monasteries and castles spread throughout the island. In 1967 the total revenue from 1·9 million tourists was $202 million, an increase of 91 per cent over 1960, tourists from Britain and Northern Ireland accounting for approximately 70 per cent of this total. Since 1967, tourism has been Ireland's largest single export, and, except for Spain and Austria, plays a more important rôle in balancing Eire's international payments than in any other European country. Tourism adds 10 per cent to the total purchasing power, and accounts for 15 per cent of all employment in Ireland.[68]

Most of this spending, employment and purchasing power is spread over a wide area of the country. Whereas 52 per cent of all industrial employment in Ireland[69] in 1961 was centred on the city of Dublin and on the counties of Dublin and Louth, these areas possess only 20 per cent of all hotel accommodation (and much of this is for non-tourists). A chain of tourist information and accommodation booking services has representatives in almost every town and in many villages. Organisationally, the Irish tourist industry is a model of efficiency. That Eire should compete successfully with southern Europe for the attention of British tourists is partly a reflection of the two countries' proximity and the former country's little-used road network, but it is also a tribute to Irish marketing methods.

These marketing methods have rested heavily upon themes 'based on the strength of the rural environment'[70] and on the Irish people as much as places. This necessarily means that the areas to which the tourist has been directed possess the most meagre of tourist facilities —that is, sanitation, entertainment, recreation, electricity and the like. The Bord Failte Eireann was established in 1955 to encourage, subsidise and occasionally direct the provision of such facilities. Indirectly, therefore, as well as directly, the general quality of rural amenity has been raised by tourism for the residential population.

In addition to providing new facilities whereby the attractions of Eire be fully enjoyed, the capacity of the attractions themselves must be weighed. This can and has been done as far as physical planning is concerned. Zoning of activities to reduce conflict and obtain a quasi-optimum use of attractions has been introduced. Since, however, the major attraction of Ireland is the way of life of the West's peasantry, the capacity of this way of life ought to be assessed also.

A study[71] suggested that in Donegal for every fifty persons a capacity of one tourist, at any one time, was desirable; for every fifty persons living in Donegal's Gaeltacht (officially recognised and subsidised Gaelic-speaking zones) an additional tourist could be absorbed; and another for every fifty traditional houses. At present tourist spending, rates and lengths of stay, this would mean that receipts from tourists, shared out under straw eaves by Gaelic speakers, would amount to $75 a year per person.

This policy, which assumes that the tourist capacity of a society is directly proportional to economic, social and cultural distance between itself and its guests, if acted upon would present problems. (And even if it is not taken as a model it nevertheless pinpoints those features which have stimulated demand in the past.) First, it directs the bulk of the tourist revenue to the most backward areas. Since the tourist is unlikely to have the Gaelic, the Gael must use English more and more. Secondly, traditional housing, by definition, cannot house large numbers of comfort-seeking foreigners. Both these goals are self-defeating.

In short, the greatest amount of economic good is being directed to those geographic areas susceptible to the greatest amount of social change. The West is poor and rigidly traditional. Bord Failte cannot sell traditionalism and cannot swell the West's purse *and* retain the honest sod roof and the Gaelic vernacular.

East Africa (Uganda, Kenya and Tanzania)

East Africa has long offered a unique product to the tourist market. Nowhere else can wild life, in abundance and great variety, be so readily viewed. At present about $60 million are spent each year by tourists to the region, Kenya receiving $36 million, Tanzania $14 million, and Uganda $10 million.[72] Over 80 per cent of tourists to

Table 3:12

Land devoted to game viewing, reserves, etc.

	National parks and marine parks (sq. miles)	Game reserves, animal sanctuaries, etc. (sq. miles)	% of total national area
Kenya	9,200	3,200	5·5%
Uganda	2,800	2,000	5%
Tanzania	11,800	21,000	9%

Source: J. Ouma.[74] op. cit.

NB: Controlled hunting areas excluded.

Uganda visit game parks during their stay and the figure is unlikely to be lower in the other countries.[73] The designation of the resources for wild-life viewing is relatively easily made: outside the present or proposed National Parks and Game Reserves, there are only a few areas which can be classified as resource potential.

The questions of the capacity of such resources and their optional management are complex. Mitchell[75] estimates that by A.D. 2000, if tourist numbers maintain their present rate of increase—15 per cent per annum—there will be more than one tourist per square mile of game-viewing area for much of the year, assuming their even distribution throughout such areas. At present this assumption does not hold true. Some parks are rarely visited, for example Rukwa in Tanzania, whilst others like Nairobi Game Park already exceed the forecast demand.

On the whole capacities are grossly under-used, and by judicious selection of new hotel sites and water-holes there is little doubt, in the present writer's opinion, that one person per square mile densities can be achieved without detraction—as far as the tourist is concerned. Such a figure would mean 750 persons (say 250 cars) on Queen Elizabeth National Park's ninety-six miles of viewing roads (excluding twenty-seven miles of through-traffic routes) at any one time, not an excessive density. More difficult problems will arise in the accommodation of these visitors. Queen Elizabeth National Park would require six or so safari lodges, each the size of the present, luxurious Mweya Lodge. In such circumstances the most advantageous locations for such lodges (for animals and employees alike) would be along the peripheries of the parks. Another solution might be the extensive development of air-taxi services from hotel complexes in the larger cities where ancillary tourist services could be readily concentrated.

At present well over half the area of East Africa cannot profitably be used for agriculture because of aridity or excessive soil moisture. Whilst semi-arid scrubland occupies most of northern and eastern Kenya and much of central and southern Tanzania, valley swamps are a feature of Uganda. In this light the percentages of land devoted to game parks in these countries take on a new aspect: is the land in game parks being efficiently utilised? Weight is given to this question by the political ideologies of Tanzania and Uganda, both of whom stress the rôle of the peasant cultivator in development and nation-building. In Kenya development planners hope to provide sufficient new employment for the expected number of would-be wage-earners.

Conflicts of interest already exist: between cattle and game in Serengeti and Ngorogoro; between industry and bird life at Nakuru; between electricity and wild life at Murchison Falls; between irrigation schemes and wildlife in the Semliki Valley.[76] For Kenya, Mitchell has estimated that $65 million investment in tourism up to 1973 will increase the Gross Domestic Product by $53 million, an increase 'in capital stock rather less than the increase necessary to secure the same increase in GDP in manufacture, and about the same necessary in agriculture'.[77] If investment returns in agriculture are comparable to those in tourism, then there cannot but be increasing conflict of interest between the two as the eight million, three-acre, hoe-cultivated peasant holdings of East Africa attempt to improve their techniques, yields and profitability.

The second major resource of East African tourism is its coastline, and it is here that the most rapid growth of the industry is being experienced. Some European countries, notably Germany and Italy, now permit low-cost package holidays to undercut regular air fares by more than 50 per cent. The result has been that coast-based holidays with safari forays to inland game parks are at present being enjoyed for as little as $300, and within five years it is very likely that this price will fall to $200 or less.[78] In this case, then, Kenyan and Tanzanian beaches will readily compete with Mediterranean resorts.

The methods utilised in marketing and developing tourism vary a great deal between the three countries. In Uganda almost all hotels are under the parastatal management of the Uganda Development Corporation. Tanzania, although encouraging private and foreign investment in this field, has attracted little of it; its nationalisation policies in respect of other industries have rather overshadowed this gesture to capitalism. Until early in 1971, Uganda's left wing policies did little to encourage foreign investment in tourism.[79] Kenya has actively encouraged such investment.

The extent of white settlement in colonial Kenya facilitated the development of tourism in that country, laying the infrastructure of international tourism in the independent nation. Roads, hotels, and ancillary entertainments were encouraged by domestic European recreational demand before 1962. Today, $6 million a year are spent on tourism by Kenyans within Kenya.[80] After Independence and re-resettlement schemes, moreover, a significant handful of European Kenyans moved into the tourist industry, running both travel agencies and hotels. Lastly, strong contacts with Britain led large numbers of settlers' relatives to pay visits to the country. All these influences have helped make Kenya the leader in East African tourism.

Future foreign participation in tourist development hinges on several questions. It has been argued that foreigners are needed to provide skilled management; to guide the industry on matters relating to likely tastes of foreign tourists, and to facilitate cooperation

C

with tourist marketing operators in the demand areas.[81] Further, foreign investment will take the risk out of national governments' hands, whilst, through judicious taxation, excessive profits accruing to such investment can be trimmed to a level considered desirable by such governments. It is estimated that, despite extensive foreign investment, Kenya retains 70 per cent of its tourist revenues and that the Kenya Government receives a rate of return of 20–30 per cent on its own investments in privately managed tourist concerns.

Yet, to many East Africans, these arguments reek of neo-colonialism. 'Skilled management' arguments have often been excuses for continued external domination. The encouragement of 'foreign tastes' is difficult to swallow in the Republics of the *wananchi*, of *ujamaa*, and of the Common Man. 'Cooperation with European marketeers' in other fields has often been interpreted as detrimental to local interests. Tourism in East Africa, therefore, represents a challenge to the region's expressed developmental emphasis and to its political ideologies.

CONCLUSIONS

Tourist resources are in principle no different from any others: one may market that for which there is an existing demand, or, by skilful invention and publicity, create a new product and/or a new form of demand. Reductions in transport costs (in this case, transport of the consumer) may radically alter the competitiveness of a product which, say, previously could not supply a known demand because of remoteness and in whose absence more accessible and therefore less costly, if less satisfactory, resources were being utilised. Coal measures' ironstone and Scarborough have more in common than meets the eye; so have Kiruna haematite and Split.

Unlike many resources, tourist attractions can be sold to many people at one time and resold to later consumers. Multiple use at one time and over time, however, does not mean that the resources are infinite. Indeed each sale modifies the resource which thus changes continually. Since cultural attractions form a major portion of tourist resources then these will be profoundly modified and in the end radically changed as sales of these commodities progress. Work on the social impact of tourism is then urgently needed. In the meantime one suspects that there is a strong case for government control over tourist development—not for economic reasons, since tourism seems to flourish under both free and controlled economic systems, but for social ones.

Lastly, the rapid rise of incomes from tourism, the geographical spread of tourists and rapidly falling relative travel costs suggest that within four or five decades geographical distance will have ceased to play an important rôle in determining tourist regions. Social distinctions, amongst tourists themselves, will then devolve more on artificial price regulation.

1. Government of Cyprus, n.d. *The Second Five Year Plan*. Nicosia.
2. Boorstein, D., 1966. *The Image*, Harmondsworth.
3. Nagenda, J., 1966. Note in *African Development*, p. 15.
4. Pouris, D., and Beerli, C., 1963. *Culture and Tourism*, OECD.
5. *Times Educational Supplement*, 10 July, 1970.
6. Skinner, J. S., 1969. Private Financing of Tourism Development in Africa, *UNECA/Dag Hammarskjold Foundation Seminar Paper*. Uppsala.
7. Fanon, F., 1968. *The Wretched of the Earth*, Harmondsworth.
8. See for example, Huxley, A., 1925. *Along the Road*. London.
9. Besson, A., 1964. Le tourisme dans la Province de Gerone, *Méditerranée*, p. 45.
10. International Union of Official Travel Organizations (IUOTO), 1968. *Economic Review of World Tourism*. Geneva.
11. German National Tourist Office (in London), n.d. *The Development of Tourism in the Federal Republic of Germany*.
12. Banca Totta-Alianca, 1968. *Portugal—some facts abouts its Economy*. Lisbon.
13. Clary, D., 1967. La fréquentation touristique sur la côte normande, *Norois*, p. 473.
14. Lande, A. B., 1965. L'activité touristique dans la région de Gréoux-les-Bains, *Méditerranée*, p. 29.
15. Mongolian Embassy in Delhi, 1969. *Mongolian Newsletter*, November.
16. Japanese National Tourist Organization, 1968. *Tourism in Japan 1967-68*. Tokyo.
17. Withington, W. A., 1961. Upland resorts and tourism in Indonesia, *Geog. Review*, p. 418.
18. Government of Cyprus. op. cit.
19. Eriksen, W., 1968. Zur geographie des fremdenverkehrs in Argentinien, *Die Erde*, p. 305.
20. Ogilvie, F. W., 1933. *The Tourist Movement*. London.
21. Waters, S. R., 1967. Trends in international tourism, *Development Digest*, vol. V, no. 2. Washington.
22. Tourists and Governments, *The Economist*, 16 March, 1969, p. 827.
23. IUOTO. op. cit.
24. Jackson, R. T., 1969. Uganda's place in world tourism, *Makerere University College, Department of Geography, Seminar Papers* (cyclostyled).
25. Government of Israel, 1968. *Investor's Guide to Tourism*. Tel Aviv.
26. Renucci, J., 1961. La Corse et le tourisme, *Rev. Géog. de Lyon*, p. 207.
27. Young, A. *Travels in France 1787-8-9*.
28. Juillard, E., 1957. La Côte des Maures, *Rev. Géog. Alp.*, p. 289.
29. Christaller, W., 1965. Geographie des fremdenverkehrs in Europa, *Tagungsbericht und wissenschaftliche Ablanlungen*. Bochum.
30. Huxley. op. cit.
31. French Embassy, 1967. *Tourist Development in Languedoc-Roussillon*. London.

32. Japanese National Tourist Organisation. op. cit.
33. Press, T., 1969. Air charter operations, *UNECA/Dag Hammarskjold Foundation Seminar Paper*. Uppsala.
34. UNO/Shankland Cox & Co., 1965. *A Tourist Development Plan for Hvar*.
35. Velev, V., Mičev, N., Dončev, D., 1969. Le devéloppement économogéographique et les problèmes de la zone des stations balnéaires Nassebar-Pomorie, *Izvestia* (Sofia), p. 199.
36. Government of Israel, op. cit.
37. Gravier, J. F., 1964. *L'Amenagement du Territoire et L'Avenir des Régions Françaises*. Paris.
38. Renucci. op. cit.
39. Joly, J., 1963. Le tourisme britannique en Savoie et en Dauphiné, *Rev. Géog. Alp.*, p. 43.
40. Gibbon, E., 1814. *Miscellaneous Works*, vol. 2.
41. Lunn, A., 1963. *The Swiss and their Mountains*. London.
42. Marion, J., and Loup, J., 1965. Cent ans de tourisme alpine, *Rev. Géog. Alp.*, p. 423.
43. Veyret, P., and Veyret, G., 1964. Petites et moyennes villes des Alpes, *Rev. Géog. Alp.*, p. 1.
44. ibid.
45. Janin, B., 1964. Tourisme dans les grandes Alpes italiennes, *Rev. Géog. Alp.*, p. 211; Janin, B., 1965. Le trafic au tunnel routier du Grand St. Bernard, *Rev. Géog. Alp.*, p. 435; Marion and Loup. op. cit.
46. Bonaface, U., 1968. Il turismo della neve in Italia, *Riv. Geog. Italiana*, p. 157.
47. Meriaudeau, R., 1967. Naissance d'une nouvelle station de sports d'hiver—Superdevoluy, *Rev. Géog. Alp.* p. 211.
48. Meriaudeau, R., 1963. Les stations de sports d'hiver en Suisse, en Autriche, et en Allemagne, *Rev. Géog. Alp.*, p. 675.
49. Billet, J., 1966. La montagne, chance du tourisme tessinois de demain, *Rev. Géog. Alp.*, p. 373.
50. Balseinte, R., 1961. L'essor récent des sports d'hiver dans le Tyrol autrichien, *Rev. Géog. Alp.*, p. 537.
51. Lunn, A. op. cit.
52. Leconte, C., 1965. Le tourisme de la neige, *Méditerranée*, p. 9.
53. Marion and Loup. op. cit.
54. Janin, 1964. op. cit.
55. Piriou, N., 1967. La 'Mittelgebirge', *Rev. Géog. Alp.*, p. 605.
56. Cribier, F., 1961. De Venosc aux Deux Alpes, *Rev. Géog. Alp.*, p. 293.
57. Bonapace. op. cit.
58. Veyret, P., and Veyret, G., 1966. Tourisme et vie rurale en montagne, *Rev. Géog. Alp.*, p. 5.
59. Pannetta, R., 1966. Spagna di oggi e di domani, *L'Universo*, p. 85; Naylon, J., 1967. Tourism: Spain's most important industry, *Geography* LII, p. 23.
60. Do Suoto, L., n.d. *The Reality of Portugal*. Lisbon.
61. Formica, C., 1965. La Costa Blanca e il suo sviluppo turisto, *Riv. Geog. Italiana*, p. 46.
62. Herbert, Lady, 1867. *Impressions of Spain in 1866*. London.
63. Besson. op. cit.
64. IUOTO. op. cit.
65. Banco Totto-Alianca. op. cit.
66. Bagnall, G., 1969(?). *Tourism and the Rural Areas* (cyclostyled report).
67. See for example Titmarsh, M. A. (alias of W. M. Thackeray), 1838, *The Irish Sketchbook*, or Chatterton, Lady G., 1839, *Rambles in the South of Ireland*.

68. Bord Failte Eireann, 1968. *Annual Report for 1967/8*. Dublin.
69. Government of Ireland, 1965. *Irish Statistical Abstract*. Dublin.
70. Bagnall. op. cit.
71. An Foras Forbartha, 1966. *Planning for Amenity and Tourism*. Dublin.
72. Mitchell, F., 1969. The value of tourism in East Africa, *Univ. Coll. Nairobi, Inst. for Development Studies, Disc. Paper*, 82.
73. Okereke, O., 1970. A preliminary study of game park lodges, *Univ. Coll. Makerere, Inst. of Social Research, Disc. Paper*, 185.
74. Ouma, JPBM, 1970. The evolution of tourism in East Africa, *University of East Africa Social Science Conference, Proceedings of*. Nairobi.
75. Mitchell. op. cit.
76. Carruthers, I. D., 1970. Irrigation Schemes in Uganda, *E. Afr. Geog. Rev.*, p. 11.
77. Mitchell, F., 1968. *The costs and benefits of tourism in Kenya*. Report to the Kenya Tourist Development Corporation, Nairobi.
78. Press. op. cit.
79. In September 1971, President Idi Amin Dada of Uganda announced that the Murchison Falls electricity scheme, initiated by the Obote government, was to be abandoned, and replaced by a scheme on the Aswa and Agago rivers, Acholi District.
80. Mitchell. op. cit.
81. Skinner. op. cit.

4

NORTH AMERICAN LEISURE

When trying to come to terms with any aspect of North America a European has to allow for an immediate and powerful expansion of scale. So it is for the European geographer, who is presented with a continent, a unit economy and culture, so that he is ill-at-ease with many of his preconceptions. At mid-century in the United States there were sixteen million retired people, the average length of the working week was forty hours, 34 per cent of total national time[1] was spent at leisure and the weeks of paid vacations totalled more than seventy million. Income levels and the increasing mobility of the American population, both difficult variables to measure but both of great importance in the recreational equation, produce a pattern of leisure activities which differs radically from the primarily European ones described in previous chapters. What to the British is a holiday abroad in terms of distance and cost is to the North American a weekend excursion to a cottage or camp site.

With these fundamental differences in scale and mobility there are also other less tangible but no less important variations in attitudes towards recreation, tourism, landscapes, cities, and wilderness areas; in fact towards all the leisure attractions which are the concern of the student of geography.

THE RELIGION OF WORK OR RECREATION

North America was settled, except for the South and the St Lawrence valley, by Europeans of a strong Calvinist tinge who traditionally had no positive attitude towards leisure as an end in itself and believed in a religion of work. Here in a new, large and relatively un-populated continent the Protestant ethic took on a powerful new edge.[2] The attitudes of the plantation South were enclosed, discarded and finally replaced towards the end of the nineteenth century by those of the more ascetic North whose ideas became the motive force in forming twentieth-century attitudes towards work and leisure in the United States.

In Canada the semi-feudal Québecois life-style was rejected by Orangeism, whose adherents directed the future of and consequently the dominant attitudes in this northern part of the continent. Thus the work ethic, which penetrated so much of Europe after the Reformation, touched the newer and less stable North American society with a greater force, and by the end of the nineteenth century had brought the promised wealth from the New World.

In 1899 Veblen discussed the results of this wealth in a less hier-archically structured society;[3] the Vanderbilts and Rockefellers built their mansions and employed their liveried servants on Fifth Avenue but looked no further than Newport, Rhode Island, and perhaps Miami, for their recreation. It was a small, literary élite who travelled: Henry James to Europe and Walt Whitman to the West.[4] Conventionally, however, the first generation of the American leisured class consumed their wealth competitively and conspicu-ously at home.

During the first and third decades of the twentieth century a num-ber of factors converged to produce the vacation in Europe.[5] The Atlantic had shrunk to a week-long pool crossed by luxury liners, the second generation of American millionaires had grown up with inherited wealth, itself a powerful disincentive to ideas of the sacred-ness of work. The canons of taste associated with conspicuous con-sumption had been adopted by so many that the mere possession of goods was no longer enough. Culture and experience were now the indices of status and they were to be found in Europe rather than North America. Had not Eliot, Pound, Scott Fitzgerald all left for Europe?[6] Were not the Parisian Left Bank and Florence's Fiesole the places to be seen? So this class of Americans began the cultural grand tour which from these few innovators has grown to a pilgrim-age of almost four million each year by the late 1960s.

At the same time a second major strain in US leisure was already apparent. If North America could not provide the cultural salvation offered by France or Italy, it could provide the spiritual salvation of the wilderness. Thoreau[7] and Whitman[8] had sanctified this peculiarly North American resource and if the tourist could not improve his mind vacationing at home, he could at least save his soul.

In response to this need, since 1872 when Yellowstone was established as the first National Park, large areas in North America have become primarily recreation resources. This development has no European precedent, as land is scarce in the more densely populated countries and open spaces are rarely used in leisure time only. During the last hundred years 'possession of these lands formed the primary basis of Federal recreation interest, whether direct as in the case of a national park or incidental as in the case of a national forest or at the Tennessee Valley Authority reservoir'.[9]

Table 4:1

Acreage acquired by US Federal Agencies through Land and
Water Conservation Funds, 1965–69

Year	National Park Service	Forest Service	Bureau of Sport, Fisheries and Wildlife
1965	729	—	—
1966	4,419	68,308	—
1967	52,596	107,051	3
1968	62,096	94,520	2,557
1969 (estimate)	102,300	103,900	732
TOTAL	222,140	373,779	3,292

Source: E. Fitch and J. E. Shanklin, 1970. *The Bureau of Outdoor Recreation*. New York.

These resources and the demands made upon them will be discussed in more detail later in the chapter, but it is important to underline here the differences between National Parks in Great Britain and other countries in Western Europe where multiple use is made of land privately owned, and North American federally owned and managed parks which are kept primarily for recreational use.

For the American the hand of man was seen as the enemy of natural beauty and the work of God. In this way a paradox was introduced. The American looked to Europe for pleasure at leisure among the works of man, and to tracts of unspoilt frontier land in America where he could escape his own works to be with God. In a sense both forms of recreation had overtones of moral uplift, the compromise necessary to the work ethic. 'Scouting has always emphasised the power of life in the open to build character.'[10]

THE AMERICAN TOURIST

With more discretionary income, leisure time, and a higher degree of mobility than any other population, North Americans play the largest role in the business of international tourism. It continues to be true that 'the American increasingly has the possibility of seeking recreation in foreign countries. Technological and economic advances have made the world, or at least the free world, more and more accessible'[11] in both a physical and economic sense.

North American tourism represents the most highly developed example of a leisure industry, and as such has been closely scrutinised by economists and other social scientists.[12] It is outdoor recreation which has been the major domestic interest however, and US tourist statistics have received scant attention from geographers. Only in 1961 was a Travel Service established as part of the Department of Commerce in an attempt to reduce the gap in the balance of United States tourist payments by encouraging more foreigners to vacation there, and more residents to take holidays at home. The majority of visitors from abroad are Canadian, since comparable standards of living and strong transport links mean that there is now one large integrated system of recreational provision in North America, which operates on the same scale as the system of international tourism in Western Europe.

However, the American tourist in the chain of Hilton Hotels is a world-wide phenomenon, and it is not surprising that the United States Government is seriously concerned by the imbalance in tourist payments effected by its nation's increasing interest in movement abroad during their annual vacation periods. Already by 1960 more than 7,233,000 trips were made by US residents into foreign countries, while only 5,600,000 trips were made into the United States from abroad. The exchange rates and relative costs of living are the main constraints affecting the development of tourism from foreign countries into the United States. Only Canada, Britain, West Germany and Japan can provide the necessary income and population which make possible a large number of holiday trips into the United States, and the European nations have a similar variety of climate, culture and landscape far closer to home. For many other nations, movement into the United States is for political, professional or business reasons only.

Canada and the United States, except where they can provide for each others' needs, are most important as the biggest market in international tourism. It would seem that 'Main Street USA' can be found all over the continent, and increasingly all over the world now, in the form of the Burger King, Kentucky Fried Chicken, Ice Cream Parlor, Sunset Strip townscape which is essentially a landscape of leisure and a monument to the commercialism that characterises the American leisure industry.

In twentieth century conditions it is proper to talk of a highly organised entertainment industry, to distinguish within it between production and distribution, to examine forces making for competition, integration and control, and to relate such study to the statistics of national income and output, the development of advertising, international economic relations, and not least to the central economic concept of the market which in the twentieth century is as much concerned with leisure as it is with work.[13]

It is perhaps because North Americans comprise such a large part of the international market, and because they act as innovators in creating new areas of demand and fashion for later tourist developments, that they are so important in a consideration of the geography of leisure.

Traditionally the Grand Tour of Europe occupied at least half the time spent by Americans travelling abroad. During the last decade, however, the Caribbean, Central and South America, the Pacific and Far East have become equally important areas of supply. In the same way that New York and Washington States look to Canada in the summer, and Texans to Mexico, so Californians face the Pacific, and with as much enthusiasm, while Florida moves to the Bahamas and farther south. Once these areas have been opened up they are available to the affluent American from any part of the country and the cult of going somewhere new continuously expands the leisure frontier across the world. Once opened, such areas become increasingly more accessible, the interest in them passes to less affluent and less innovative tourists while the searchers for the new and the unique pass on to the next area to be introduced into the cycle.

But the essential change in the nature of tourism over the last hundred years is the sheer increase in the numbers of tourists and the expansion of the scale on which they operate (see Chapter 3). Whereas the Americans described by Henry James and Scott Fitzgerald were few and very wealthy, the latter-day tourist spends less, demands that the vacation is foreign but not too foreign and that the basic amenities offered by the affluent domestic leisure industry are provided by even the small hotels of the more remote and less developed tourist areas. He is no longer an innovator in the way that the heroes of James's novels were, but in his travels effects change over a much wider area and in so doing dilutes the resource that originally attracted him there.

The Bahamas have recently been invaded by cruise ships which sail the short trip from Miami filled with 'day trippers' seeking a holiday where 'one can drink the water, a prerequisite for many American tourists; where there is no language barrier, and where there is an aura of safety reinforced by the prim-looking constabulary in white jackets and pith helmets'.[14]

In their search for the new and the different they demand the familiarity of that which they wish to leave behind. Despite the fact that 25 per cent more Americans visited Europe in 1965 than in 1964, and that Canadians spend $3,000 million each year abroad, they increasingly fail to find the new and the different which are the main stimulus to their travel. Although diversity must still remain the key to recreational travel for many Americans, 'to the extent that the world becomes homogenised, by definition diversity is diminished and the stimulus to recreational travel is weakened'.[15]

Carrying this argument to its logical conclusion, E. M. Forster prophesied a world where 'Peking was just like Shrewsbury. Men seldom moved their bodies, all unrest was concentrated in the soul.'[16] Herein lies the dilemma between development and conservation in the provision of all kinds of facilities for recreation, a dilemma which still faces Americans within their own continent.

AMERICAN OUTDOOR RECREATION

If the American abroad has acted as an erosive agent in changing the resource base of international tourism, then to a much greater extent he has been a destructive force in the provision of outdoor recreation at home. 'One dimension of affluence and leisure in North America is mobility, and it is the mobility of the urban population across the nation which elevates outdoor recreation to the status of an important national problem.'[17] In 1900 only 40 per cent of the population of the United States was urban, but it is estimated that during the last thirty years, when the national figure has increased by about three million per year, the urban percentage has reached almost 80 per cent.[18]

If outdoor recreation can be defined as 'those leisure-time activities undertaken in relatively small groups in a rural setting'[19] then a higher concentration of people in towns means a greater separation of the demand for and the supply of resources for leisure indoors. If the market is located in the large and growing metropolitan areas, the urban dweller becomes alienated from the rural setting which is described as a vital ingredient in the recreational equation. The problems on a local scale are complex and have been described at length by urban planners.[20]

However, the degree of mobility which is an integral part of the American search for the great outdoors[21] and the wilderness means that recreational planning is more than a local or a regional problem. It has to be seen first of all on a national and in fact on an international scale since the Canadian border is no greater barrier to movement than an inter-state line within the USA.

By definition, outdoor recreation resources are located far from most of the 200 million inhabitants of the United States for these lie in the wilderness environment demanded; the function of the Bureau of Outdoor Recreation since its creation in 1963 has been 'to reclaim and protect the outdoor environment, and provide outdoor recreation opportunities'.[22] It represents the Federal interest in conservation and development of national resources for leisure which include forests, parks, wilderness areas, reservations, historic monuments and all lands federally owned and managed either wholly or partially for recreational purposes.

The development of the National Parks Service during the last fifty years in many ways epitomises the history of North American attitudes to land for leisure. In 1916 the Service was established as essentially a land-management and water-resource control agency. Most of the Parks, which are located in every part of the country but more in the West than the heavily populated areas of the North East, are areas of outstanding beauty or scientific interest, such as Death Valley, California, and the Grand Canyon in Arizona. The richness of these resources for recreational purposes is reflected in continuing Federal concern for their development, and the attractiveness and accessibility of the Parks are shown by an annual growth rate of 10 per cent in number of visitors; from one million visitors to all federally controlled areas in 1920, to a total in the late 1960s which reached and exceeded 100 million.[23] The resultant overcrowding of the more popular sites or 'honey-pots' in, for example, Yosemite has raised the problem of how access and development can be allowed in the interests of long-term conservation in all of the thirty-three Parks. Much of the thirteen million acres of Federal land has been deprived of its natural beauty through development, especially since the last war. It is an old and familiar problem, a conflict between the need to develop and make available more land for outdoor leisure and the need to conserve areas which are irreplaceable.

The wilderness

A more recent development at the Federal level was the approval by Congress of the Wilderness Act of 1964. At least nine million acres of National Forest land were designated as the first legally protected

American wilderness. After a long preoccupation with this concept and an extensive literature on the subject,[24] the United States finally committed large tracts of land (minimum area for a wilderness area is 5,000 acres) to freedom from economic or any other form of exploitation. Many reasons were given and long debates followed on the need to define the wilderness by making preservation orders.[25] The Act marked the culmination of a century of attempts by geographers and others to persuade the nation of the state of crisis in the preservation of pristine America.[26] The Nixon Administration since 1968 has exalted the cause of conservation, together with the anti-pollution campaign, to the status of wartime emergency. Whatever the motives which lie behind this new concern, there can be no doubt that the nation will benefit.

It has been suggested that 'the significant history of outdoor recreation in the United States begins, not with the wilderness, but with its decline'.[27] Certainly the beginnings of conservation in North America coincided with the writings of mid-nineteenth-century Malthusians[28] and it is to be hoped that the new concern can be sustained after the renewed efforts of the early 1960s.[29] The interest in wilderness rather than simply non-urban areas stems from a number of causes and is particularly American. The myth of the frontier, the wholesale destruction of so many parts of the American continent by rapacious economic development and the biblical overtones of so much of American life have all contributed to the idea that 'in wilderness lies the preservation of the world'.[30] The myth has been sanctified by Thoreau, has survived in the American mind, and has found renewed interest in the 1960s flight of so many Americans from the realities of the post-industrial state. Naturally it has become a leitmotive of American outdoor leisure being, as it is, the result of so many strains in American life and recreation. It is seen anew in the Canadian myths of the Great North and the Arctic wilderness.

Traditionally the Americans have led the field of outdoor recreational planning, but in recent times the Canadians have put forward some rigorous proposals for land-use zoning in Federal and Provincial Parks.[31] In some ways their problems of provision and access are more acute. Two thirds of Canada's population is concentrated in heavily urbanised areas within one hundred miles of the north shores of Lakes Erie and Ontario, both potentially major recreational resources badly damaged by water pollution. However, the present areas of supply are in the far north, the East Coast and the Western Cordilleran regions, all regions of low population density and difficult access. Those lands which are relatively accessible are intensively used, suffering problems from the conflict between public and private development and conservation, while large tracts in more remote areas, such as Wood Buffalo Park in the North West Territory, are too far from centres of demand and are underused.

THE CANADIAN SITUATION

In the nineteen national parks created since 1885 the emphasis has been on a form of *laissez faire* development which has left many of them in an unfortunate state of disrepair. Ontario, as the most populous province, has suffered more than others, and in response to a situation of overuse has evolved a complex system of land-use zoning which attempts to reconcile Federal, provincial and regional and local conflicts.[32]

Table 4:2

Acreage of Canadian land in 1967 administered by
Parks Authorities

State	National Parks[1]	Provincial Parks[2]
Ontario	879,500	10,100,000
British Columbia	3,300,000	6,100,000
Alberta	3,400,000	4,000,000
Saskatchewan ⎫		1,800,000
Quebec ⎪	3,300,000	1,700,000
New Brunswick ⎬		1,600,000
and others ⎭		

Sources: [1]National Parks Service, 1964. *National Parks Policy.* Ottawa. [2]*Classification of Provincial Parks*, 1967. Toronto.

The history of National Parks in Canada reveals that the rôles of educator and entertainer have been most important in the minds of policy-makers, and for this reason, among others, recreational planning has been piecemeal.[33] Perhaps in reacting against this *ad hoc* development Ontarian planners have moved rapidly towards a conservative approach which places the wilderness concept in a new and much stronger position in their list of recreational priorities. Federal interests are relatively small in Ontario, and the Department of Lands and Forests administers ninety-seven provincial parks which range from five-acre picnic areas to Algonquin Park, an immensely varied and large area of public land (2,000 sq. miles) on the edge of the Canadian Shield. The Department classifies its land in five different ways.[34] 'Primitive Parks' are essentially wilderness areas which will provide for the 'psychological need of many people to know that unspoiled wilderness areas exist'. It would seem that, in using these Parks intended particularly for 'wildland recreation', Canadians bring with them so many of the trappings of civilisation in the form of heating, refrigeration and entertainment that the idea of the wilderness as a frontier zone in which a new form of life is possible is never transferred from the realms of imagination and fantasy into reality. Thoreau saw the wilderness as a place where it is possible to reject and escape from organised society, bureaucracy and order. From work done more recently it has been discovered that 'for a minority of people the appeal of outdoor recreation may lie in the possibility of getting away from people to nature and solitude, but for the majority a main attraction of outdoor recreation seems to be the opportunity to be with people and share leisure opportunities . . .'.[35]

This has important implications for the geographer. Outdoor recreation must be rural, but not too much so in that it must be accessible to a fairly large number of people. In the Ontarian classification, as an alternative to wilderness areas, there are also 'Recreation Parks' which are user-oriented, instead of resource-based. They provide camping facilities, day-use activities, beaches and swimming areas, and are by definition near to population centres from which they are intensively used. Their locational pattern is related to the market in southern Ontario, Quebec and the Mid-West of the USA, and resource requirements are minimal; water, a certain amount of afforestation for shade on campsites, and ease of access from major routeways.

The public pattern of provision for outdoor recreation in North America is therefore dichotomous. There are resource-based facilities, the location of which depends upon physical determinants of historical events. Most Federal recreational interests fall into this category since they aim to 'preserve for all times areas which contain significant geographical, geological, biological or historical features as a national heritage for the benefit of the people'.[36]

Provincial and local authorities are more concerned with providing space for outdoor activities which is above all accessible to urban populations. Whereas the United States Government is protecting game in Arizona so that the annual vacationer may see a particular ecological phenomenon, the New York City administration is aware that 'the open countryside is barely accessible to the people who need it most for recreation'.[37] In 1960, 53 per cent of the city's population had no cars, and public transport brought only the Long Island resorts within range of the low-income ghetto families of downtown Manhattan or the Bronx. It was estimated that there are one million New Yorkers who, because of their place of residence and relative poverty and lack of mobility, 'must patronise crowded beaches or depend on friends to secure access to non-urban recreation'.[38]

If it is true that 'the principal condition which determines the availability of outdoor recreation for residents of large metropolitan centres is encompassed in the term "access" ',[39] then municipal authorities are faced with the need to provide facilities within urban areas at a number of different levels. If federal and provincial planning for leisure has been piecemeal during this century, then local expenditure within cities has been more so. In a recent study of user-oriented facilities which are found close to the homes of the recreationally active, it was suggested that the history of city spending on parks would be a suitable barometer for measuring the history of general urban provision.[40] This kind of approach to problems of leisure in the city is symptomatic of predominant American attitudes to nature, man and the urban environment. When the city park was first introduced as an integral part of the 'city beautiful' movement in urban design history which appeared in the 1870s,[41] it was intended to be a facsimile of a rural landscape bringing 'tranquillity and rest to the mind'. These attitudes are still appearing in contemporary recreational literature[42] which in turn is used in the decision-making processes which precede metropolitan planning.[43]

The centre or the fringe?

The main leisure resource in urban areas is still seen as the park whether it be a large tract available to the population of the whole city as is Central Park to New Yorkers, Grant Park in Chicago and High Park in Toronto, or the local park consisting of one block of land grassed over, surrounded by flower-beds and accommodating a children's playground. Too often these are seen only as areas where the people trapped in the city through poverty, disability or mere misfortune can escape from the works of man and find moral and spiritual uplift away from the streets; they are simply the *rus in urbe*, the ideal of the urban planner. The other major form of publicly provided urban recreation has been the large cultural centre in the heart of the city wherein are grouped theatres, art galleries and concert halls. Both forms of provision, outdoor and indoor, have been attacked on the grounds that they do not give an adequately varied base to the service being offered, especially for the dispossessed who form the nucleus of demand for public and centrally placed amenities.[44] The main problems facing most American cities in their planning for leisure have been, first, the anachronistic and puritanical attitudes towards what should be provided, and second and perhaps more important the recurrent, severe lack of money allocated for recreational expenditure. The flight to the suburbs, which lie outside the boundaries of the city as an administrative and therefore financial unit, has taken a large slice from the city's income. Central facilities are used by the population of the whole city region, many of whom do not pay taxes to the authority which must finance these local developments. Federal or State money may be obtainable for large prestige projects like art galleries but it is far more difficult to obtain if the development is more mundane but no less expensive. Sports stadia, swimming pools and other large-scale community facilities require subsidies if they are to operate successfully in the provision of alternative leisure amenities for central city residents who are often deprived by low income, inadequate transport facilities and educational opportunities from the activities which are accessible to the more affluent, mobile suburbanite.

That this may be overcome in part is shown by the case of Metropolitan Toronto, set up in 1951 as a blueprint for North American urban regional government, and discussed in more detail later in this chapter. Here the suburbs have been included within the metropolitan region and may subsidise the provision of free swimming pools, summer outdoor sports, open ice-rinks in winter, well-kept local parks and a variety of other amenities for the poorer centre-city residents. This form of government, together with similar enlightened attitudes, has produced a well-serviced and well-used network of publicly provided leisure in Toronto, in Teesside (see Chapter 8), but in few other North American or British metropolitan areas. The problem of provision in the suburbs of large American cities is very different from that in the more densely populated West European city. They cover a much larger area, have grown up as private developments in a period when profit is more important than providing services. While they reflect the continuing demand of the North American for escape from the dirt and noise of the city to the purer, cleaner, healthier rural (or at least extra-urban) fringe, and provide more open space for larger families, they offer little more than church and shopping plaza in terms of extra-domestic activities. The response is to leave them at weekends for the cottage, or in the evening for the cinemas and theatres of the downtown area. Many are reluctant to make the long commuter trip again after a day in the city and resort to at-home recreation with do-it-yourself kits, stereo equipment and television sets that eventually replace the concert hall and community centre, and create an aura of self-containment in leisure time which is the hallmark of the suburban household in other areas of the American life-style. More decentralisation of recreational facilities will be needed to alleviate the problem of isolation and social deprivation which is an acknowledged result of long days spent alone in the suburbs. There is obviously a demand for more local amenities as shown by the formation of local housewives' clubs, increasing crime rates among bored adolescents who live in affluent suburbs far from the attraction of city-centre provision, and for the retired with a great deal of time to spare. The method of providing local centres with libraries, small theatres, and other social and community activities in such areas has been suggested by Carver.[45] Proposals to build mobile arts centres which can be toured in the out-of-town areas have been put forward by the American Association of Arts Councils, which is very concerned to increase the accessibility of all art forms to a wider public, and to encourage a greater degree of involvement. The idea of taking part rather than watching is gaining ground as shown by recent figures published in *The Culture Consumers* by Alvin Toffler.

The sociology of leisure in urban areas is highly complicated and under-researched. The American city has never had the public plazas and community street life that pass for leisure in European cities, except perhaps among the recent European emigrants to them. The preoccupation with privacy, individuality and work that characterises so much of American life has had its impact upon leisure provision as a public service, so that both the urban poor and the suburban rich suffer from inadequate facilities for recreation in towns. The example of Toronto's metropolitan area, and its attempts to solve these problems, has already been mentioned and will be examined in more detail now.

Metropolitan Toronto: a prototype in provision for leisure
The City of Toronto, a Mid-West American city in many respects and the product of the last 170 years, is a good illustration of both the problems and the successes of public provision for leisure in the North American city. Since it is the second Canadian city with a population of 2·2 million, it has perhaps more advantages in respect of national interests and funds than US cities of a similar size. However, it is taken as an example in so far as it illustrates many of the attitudes that characterised the American city of the nineteenth and early twentieth centuries, and at present represents some of the principles of recreational provision that it would be well to apply to cities such as Washington DC, Chicago, Philadelphia, Baltimore, and nearer home, in Montreal.

The city was settled in the first decade of the nineteenth century by Loyalists who crossed from the United States after the War of Independence. They were a small group and while they represented to a degree the English gentleman's idea of leisure and patronage in such activities as horse-racing, hunting, fishing, etc., they were soon swamped both in numbers and influence by the Lowland Scottish and Ulster Protestants who settled in Ontario from the 1830s.

The city in the mid-nineteenth century was dominated by men with a penchant for hard work and a dislike of such immoral pursuits as drinking and gaming, common in this city as in many frontier towns at the time. Leisure was taken in summer by swimming in the lake off the wharves or on the island that formed the harbour, and in winter by skating and lacrosse, a game first introduced to the Canadian by the Indians and later exported to the United States.[46] Cricket was the badge of the Englishness of Toronto. But all these were private forms of leisure and there was no hint of public provision until 1840, when Garrison Commons was created as the first city park. During the 1850s there was a long and involved discussion as to whether the waterfront which was owned by the city should be laid out as a pleasure promenade for the citizens.

This controversy, which ended with the railway being laid along the city's waterfront and thereby alienating public land from public use, is symptomatic of the attitude of Toronto and of most American cities at that time, when the profit motive was dominant and few parks could be justified on economic grounds. The only break in this process was during the 'city beautiful' movement when a delegation of Toronto city fathers made a trip to Buffalo and Detroit to assess provision of parks etc. there. But little came of it. After the bequest of High Park, a former estate park to the west of the city, the municipal park system became a reality in 1884 with the appointment of a superintendent of parks and recreation who was responsible for the management of all publicly owned lands designated for these purposes, and defended their use on grounds of health and welfare: 'lungs for the city'. Only in this way could parks be justified, and never on the grounds of the need for recreational provision alone.

The same attitude gradually removed the inns and taverns from the city in the later part of the century. The famous appellation of 'Toronto The Good' springs from the strong temperance fervour that abolished such places of leisure from the town so that the work ethic rooted itself deeply in the minds of Torontonians. Theatres and opera houses were generally frowned upon and although by World War II the population had risen to one million, there was serious underprovision for leisure, especially in the public sector.

During the 1950s and even more during the last decade, there has been a fundamental change in attitudes towards recreational activity in Canada as a whole, in Ontario, and especially in Toronto, which is now an affluent and booming city. It is acutely aware of its growing challenge to Montreal as the dominant city in Canada, and with a large population of new Italian and Commonwealth immigrants, the city has developed one of the best organised and broadly based systems of public urban leisure provision in North America. At the same time the private demand for holiday and short period leisure has grown as affluence and less restricted attitudes towards leisure have appeared.

Since the early years of this century emphasis has been laid on community provision in the city, and with this on welfare rather than recreation. The Toronto Playground Association was formed in 1911 to cater for the needs of each neighbourhood, and the system grew to include forty-eight playgrounds in 1925, eighty-two in 1945 and 216 in 1969.[47] The most important aspect of this development was the immediate accessibility of the areas to all people in the city. The amenities were free, distributed throughout all, and particularly the less affluent, areas of the urban core, and the Department of Parks and Recreation now follows a policy of providing all public facilities at this local level without charge.

It was calculated that at a cost of $30,000 in wages, only $75,000 would be received from payments at the doors of all outdoor and indoor pools, community centres and other basic recreational amenities, and this profit did not seem large enough to justify limiting access to those who could afford to pay. The facilities are used to capacity. In the summer of 1970, ten outdoor swimming pools, seventy-four wading pools and fifteen indoor pools were available to, and well patronised by, schools and casual users. Musical and other events in the parks were well attended, and although Ontario's climate means that maintenance costs are lower than for similar indoor activities in Great Britain, the philosophy underlying this breakthrough in recreational provision is one which should be studied by all who are involved in similar administration positions.

At a time when the British Government is planning to introduce museum charges, the policy in Metropolitan Toronto is enviable. Despite its Puritan beginnings, there is a great deal of truth in the belief that this kind of community provision should be part of contemporary health, welfare and leisure expenditure. If the environment of urban America is to be improved

it is not possible to isolate the problem of leisure from the concept of the set of man's life. . . . The everyday urban leisure must be an integral part of the conception of the city itself and become more and more a

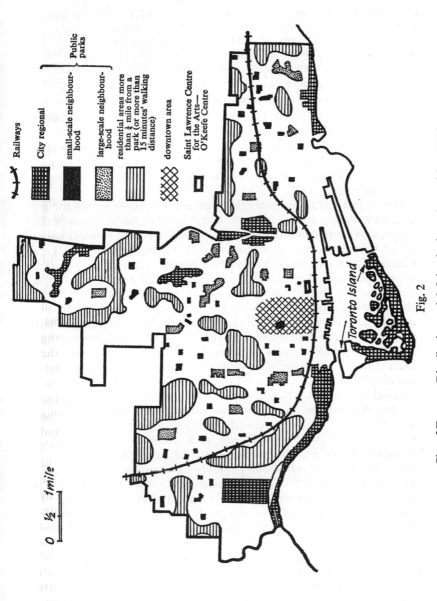

Railways

Public parks
{
City regional
small-scale neighbour-hood
large-scale neighbour-hood
}

residential areas more than ¼ mile from a park (or more than 15 minutes' walking distance)

downtown area

Saint Lawrence Centre for the Arts—O'Keefe Centre

Toronto Island

0   ½   1 mile

Fig. 2

City of Toronto. Distribution and deficiencies in park provision, 1966

Source: Proposals for a new plan for Toronto by the City of Toronto Planning Board, 1966

determinant component of its structure. The weekly suburban leisure rhythms, the relation between town and country creates the balance of occupation and utilisation of Earth. The seasonal-regional leisure, the 'holiday', closely determined by climatic and geographic data, becomes increasingly a predominant component for the planning of the territory.[48]

The Department of Recreation for the city of Toronto now operates a current budget of approximately $7·5 million, which does not include money spent on construction of new facilities and land acquisitions.[49] Development of large-scale facilities in the city centre has also been extensive during the 1960s, and the metropolitan area is now served by two large arts centres (St Lawrence and O'Keefe), the Royal Alexandria theatre which seats 1,500, and a small repertory Playhouse.

It remains clear, however, that the main concern is still for increased provision at the local level and it is the stated intention of the policy-makers to continue to acquire land for neighbourhood parks which will allow each citizen to live within fifteen minutes' walking distance (or a quarter of a mile) of a recreational facility. Figure 2 shows the areas where more land is needed for open space. These parks and playgrounds do not provide only for children, but also for the old and disabled, the isolated housewife, the energetic adolescent and the disoriented, newly arrived immigrant. What is perhaps more significant is the undeniable fact that it is those who are most in need, in every sense, who gain most from the use of these areas. During the day they are filled with children under school age using the attractive, brightly coloured slides and swings. At lunchtime the small child is replaced by the worker who has left the office with sandwiches in search of grass, trees and sunshine in the fresh air to recover from the strains of central heating or air-conditioning. In the summer the neighbourhood park is a place to sunbathe in the crowded, residential apartment areas of inner-city Toronto and throughout school vacations supervision is provided at the city's expense for school-children who learn new games and skills out of doors. It is, however, during the evenings and at weekends that the playgrounds and parks, like the pools and rinks, are best used by those who are less mobile and need space in the city when at leisure. In immigrant areas of Toronto the local park is the Italian piazza, and there is noise and activity on the pavements around it which adds a new dimension to the previously car-dominated American street scene. In many respects the densely populated central residential areas for lower income groups are the gayer, more interesting parts of the city, and the more expensive suburban fringe seems gloomy, silent, and uninviting by comparison.

Perhaps the Toronto park may be equated in its community function and leisure provision to the English pub. Certainly indoor leisure of a type provided by the pub in England is still seriously underprovided in the city. This is to a degree the result of the temperance tradition but such places lie well within the sphere of private development, especially now that the laws controlling such places of leisure have been considerably relaxed. The major point here is that a hierarchy of leisure facilities from local provision to provision for the whole of the metropolitan area exists and is publicly controlled and freely offered.

Provision of less local, more city-wide facilities consists of parks, picnic areas and arts centres and museums. In the heart of the city, near the waterfront, a new arts complex is being built up around the O'Keefe Centre, a building originally constructed by a brewery but taken over by the city and made available for major theatre, opera, orchestral and other musical events. Next door to this is the St Lawrence Centre for the Arts which has concert hall, cinema and workshop facilities also. Nearby is the old St Lawrence Hall used for public meetings and opposite this is the cathedral. While these buildings are near each other, they do not form a centre which has been hermetically sealed from the life of the streets, as in New York's Lincoln Centre. In the same few blocks of the city centre are two markets, shipping firms and offices so that street life exists around the leisure centre and lunchtime concerts are provided free with cheap lunches for workers in the downtown area.

Another major focus in the city-wide public leisure provision is the new City Hall. This building, itself a major point of interest for visitors, has a large piazza laid out in front of it in which fountains play on a pool which in winter provides free skating and music for citizens. The square is filled with seats and flower beds among which people may sit or stroll while free concerts in the open air are given for their entertainment.

Peripheral to the city, a series of large parks provide for outdoor recreation and offer a place to visit for the day. Some are linear gorges giving recreational access to the north of the city centre and another is Toronto Island, always a source of pleasure for local citizens and laid out by successive plans during the present century into parks, picnic areas and pleasure grounds with a beach for would-be swimmers in the lake. This is cheaply accessible to the city by ferry but far enough away to provide escape from the dirt and noise to purer air and the illusion of broad horizons across the lake.

In general, Toronto provides the basic leisure facilities for all of its citizens, and especially the poorer ones, and provides them free of charge. This is in striking contrast to most North American cities, and also to European cities, and offers guidelines for urban policy in the provision of leisure within the city for those who have not the time or the wealth to escape from the urban environment, or pay for their leisure privately. Here public and private provision complement each other in a way that is all too rare in most cities.

The weekend cottage

It is mainly where public and private interests meet and in many ways conflict that most interest has been concentrated. Where a resource is scarce, and land in southern Ontario becomes increasingly so, there is often strong public pressure to restrict, and in some cases exclude, commercial provision. The cottage leisure industry in Canada has provided an alternative to the national park in the rural recreational provision and the Lakes area to the north and north-east of the city of Toronto is a particularly attractive region for weekend and vacation retreats. The acquisition of some of the best recreational land by private companies for cottage development has posed a problem ever since World War II. Canadians must now compete with Americans for plots of land in Ontario, and between 1969 and 1970 there was a 15 per cent increase in acreage of land sold by the Provincial Government to private citizens from the USA.[50]

But a critical stage of development has now been reached in the more accessible and therefore more highly developed areas near Toronto, especially around Lake Simcoe and the Muskoka Lakes where lake shores are alienated by cottage owners from the public as a whole. Campers and those visiting trailer parks are thus denied access to fishing and swimming areas, so that the variety of recreational activities in these areas is being severely diminished. Since 1964 the Department of Lands and Forests in Ontario has sold 5,830 waterfront cottage lots, and 'a wilderness area has very limited value if no one can enjoy it except wealthy sportsmen, often American'.[51] By statute, 25 per cent of Crown Land in Ontario must be retained for public use, and because of increasing land-use demands from a growing, affluent, mobile population future practice will be to reserve 40 to 50 per cent for public access. Best beaches should and will be kept for common use, while others nearby become the property of private owners. It is clear, however, that 'the summer cottage remains the single, most common characteristic and desired place of recreation for the people of Ontario and for the vacationing visitors from beyond its borders'.[52]

To restrict the alienation of land is only one part of the solution to increasing demand for land. The Canadian Shield is large by any standards, even those of North America. Californians, looking for a new frontier in which to escape from the city, have moved north and have become part of the summer human migration into northern Ontario. Access is still a problem, and better roads to the north of settled Ontario must be provided, so that overspill from the highly developed and relatively overcrowded southern fringe of the Shield can be accommodated in empty areas farther from the urbanised North East, the Great Lakes peninsular and the Middle West. While those living in these relatively local areas may not be prepared to move so far as the more northerly part of the Shield, the visitors who come from as far as California will be perfectly willing to make the extra miles in order to find relative isolation, as long as access is easy.

PRIVATE PROVISION

The private sector of recreational provision has been described as a universe unknown. In America it is not only unknown but it is almost certainly indefinable. The entire transport network of the continent must be recognised as a landscape of leisure, in fact as soon as the traveller leaves home he is subjected to a constant barrage of services, all of which, at the same time, are part of the leisure industry. In this way it is necessary to include the entire motorway network of the United States and Canada, with the omniscient motel, Howard Johnson sign and all the associated drive-in facilities of North American freeways in a study of the geography of American leisure.

The Bureau of Outdoor Recreation, in an effort to assess the extent and nature of private provision in the United States, commissioned a report which was published in 1966.[53] This included a study of camps of all kinds, picnic areas, marinas, golf courses, trailer sites, cottages, shooting ranges, ski-ing and all areas privately owned and used for outdoor recreation. They included only motels and hotels with swimming pools in their attempt to assess one type of private provision, but even so the income was totalled in billions of dollars, the enterprises in hundreds of thousands, and the main point illustrated by this work was the enormous problem involved in assessing the private sector of the recreation industry. If the report showed a $2,696,000,000 gross annual income for 132,000 enterprises, then the scale of provision when outdoor experiences are both publicly and privately supplied by caterers in National Parks and by corporations operating on all inter-state highways is beyond the scope of this study. It was estimated that public expenditure on US outdoor re-creation in 1960 was $1,150,800,000, and these figures illustrate the differences between the North American and the European situations. Whereas tourism in Europe may approach saturation point soon, the North American can still look to new areas of development at home.

A road network in the Canadian Shield is an expensive proposition if it is to be for recreational purposes only. The area has mineral resources, however, and exploitation of these is limited at present by their relative inaccessibility. Better transportation links would bring the Yukon and North West Territory further into the economic system of North America as a whole and the Canadian Government recognises the need to develop its own resources now before 'Nixon drinks Canada Dry'. Multiple use of wilderness areas has its own dangers as well as its advantages, and mineral exploitation is hardly compatible with the conservation of ecological climaxes and wild life. However, for many years in Britain forests have been successfully used as multiple use areas of both recreational and economic importance and reservoirs are already being administered in the same way.

This chapter cannot hope to do more than point some of the themes that exist in the geography of leisure in North America. Both the subject itself and the literature that has been published on it there are vast. Differences in scale of recreation and all that these differences reflect in the North American way of life lead beyond quantitative and into qualitative differences between European and North American patterns of leisure. However, as Europe increases in affluence and integrates into a continental economic and social system, then many of the problems already facing those who administer recreational planning on the North American continent will appear on this side of the Atlantic.

1. Clawson, M., 1960. *Leisure and the National Time Budget*. Resources for the Future. Washington D.C.
2. Weber, M., 1930. *The Protestant Ethic and the Spirit of Capitalism*, trans. Talcott Parsons. Boston, Mass.
3. Veblen, T., 1899. *The Theory of the Leisure Class*. New Haven, Conn.
4. As Henry James shows in his stories of Americans abroad in Europe, *Portrait of a Lady* and *Daisy Miller*.
5. An American novelist who also captured much of the spirit of the age and place in *Tender is the Night* was F. Scott Fitzgerald.
6. T. S. Eliot, Ezra Pound, Scott Fitzgerald were but a handful of the substantial number of Americans, writers, artists and intellectuals who moved to Europe in the early years of the twentieth century, feeling that their work could prosper better in a European intellectual and physical environment.
7. Thoreau, H. D., 1962. *Walden and other writings*. Toronto.
8. Whitman, W., 1891. *Leaves of Grass*. London and New York.

9. Fitch, E., and Shanklin, J. E., 1970. *The Bureau of Outdoor Recreation*. New York.
10. Mead, M., 1962. Outdoor recreation in the context of emerging American cultural values: background considerations, *Outdoor recreation resources review commission study report no. 18*. ORRRC, Washington D.C.
11. *ORRRC Study Report no. 1*, 1962. Washington D.C.
12. Clawson, M. and Knetsch, J. L., 1966. *Economics of outdoor recreation*. Baltimore.
13. Briggs, A., 1960. *Mass entertainment. The origins of a modern industry*. Adelaide.
14. *New York Times*, 23 August 1970.
15. Wolfe, R. I., 1968. Recreational travel, the new migration, *Geographical Bulletin*, vol. 9, no. 4.
16 Forster, E. M., 1928. The machine stops, in *The eternal moment and other stories*. New York.
17. Perloff, H. S., and Wingo, L., 1962. Urban growth and the planning of outdoor recreation, *ORRRC Study report no. 18*. Washington D.C.
18. ibid., p. 83.
19. *ORRRC Study Report no. 1*, 1962. Washington D.C. p. 1.
20. Gans, H. J., 1957. *Recreational planning for leisure behaviour. A goal-oriented approach*. Unpublished thesis, University of Pennsylvania.
21. Haggett, P. 1965. *Locational analysis in human geography*. London.
22. Bureau of outdoor recreation (BOR), 1967. *Federal outdoor recreational programs*. Washington D.C.
23. Memorandum from Stuart L. Udall to the Director of the US National Parks Service, 1964.
24. *ORRRC Study Report no. 3*, 1962. Washington D.C.
25. Simmons, I. G., 1966. The wilderness in mid-twentieth century America, *Town Planning Review*, no. 36, pp. 249–56.
26. Leighly, J. (Ed.), 1963. *Land and Life: A selection from the writings of Carl Ortwin Sauer*. University of California.
27. Fitch, E. M., and Shanklin, J. E. op. cit., p. 9.
28. Lowenthal, D., 1958. *George Perkins Marsh—Versatile Vermonter*. New York.
29. Udall, S. L., 1962. *The quiet crisis*. New York.
30. Ballantine Books, 1964. *In Wilderness is the Preservation of the World*. San Francisco.
31. The University of Calgary Studies in Land Use History and Landscape Change, 1969. *The Canadian National Parks: Today and Tomorrow*, National Parks Series no. 3.
32. ibid.
33. National Parks Service, 1964. *National Parks Policy*. Ottawa.
34. Department of Recreation, Ontario, 1967. *Classification of Provincial parks*. Toronto.
35. *ORRRC Study Report no. 19*, 1962. Washington DC.
36. Ottawa, 1964. op. cit.
37. *ORRRC Study Report no. 21*, 1962. Washington DC.
38. ibid.
39. ibid.
40. Clawson, M., 1962. A systems approach to the study of outdoor recreation, in *ORRRC Study Report no. 18*. Washington DC.
41. Olmsted, F. L., 1870. *Public Parks and the enlargement of towns*. Cambridge, Mass.

42. Gans, H., 1962. Outdoor recreation and mental health in *ORRRC Study Report no. 18*. Washington DC.
43. New York Regional Planning Association, 1960. *The race for open space.*
44. Jacobs, J., 1958. *The Death and Life of Great American Cities.* New York.
45. Carver, M., 1962. *Cities in the suburbs.* Toronto.
46. Dulles, F. R., 1952. *America learns to play. A history of recreation.* New York.
47. City of Toronto Department of Arts and Recreation, 1970. *Parks and recreational development, 1860–1969.* Toronto.
48. Candilis, G., 1967. *Environment and policy.* Indiana University Press, Bloomington and London.
49. Toronto, 1970. op. cit.
50. *Toronto Daily Star*, 11 July 1970.
51. ibid.
52. Ontario Historical Society, 1968. *The changing pattern of tourism in Ontario.*
53. Bureau of Outdoor Recreation, 1966. *The private sector of outdoor recreation enterprises.* Washington DC.

5

RECREATION IN RURAL BRITAIN

All over Europe rural depopulation has been a chronic demographic feature for the past century. However, there are clear indications that in some countries this trend is in the process of reversal—notwithstanding a continuing decline in the numbers employed in agricultural occupations. After a long period of polarisation of population within fairly compact urban areas, population is becoming more diffusely distributed in semi-urban regions. It would appear that any national recreational policy based on any form of land-use zoning would therefore be most readily accomplished now, before the spread of rural-urban populations makes such delimitation impossibly difficult.

It is in this setting that increasing demands on the countryside for recreation are being made.[1] It is, however, important to recognise that these demands occupy a continuum[2] which cannot be divided into rural or urban categories entirely; that developments in one part of the recreational spectrum will impinge indirectly on other activities—supply of better urban amenities may reduce pressure on rural resources; that 'there is no "national" recreational man';[3] and that in attempting to satisfy or forecast demand 'it is an inherent danger . . . that change in taste and fashion will reverse what appears to be the logical trend'.[4] Some of the major problems of recreation in rural areas are, then, its complexity, its multi-faceted nature and its apparent unpredictability—and our ignorance of it.

If this is the case, is planning for rural recreation possible at all? In the study of agriculture, it is generally agreed that, under present technological conditions, shifting cultivation is inefficient: a bare subsistence is obtained at high cost to the environment. Transport and technical development have allowed agricultural areas in the more advanced economic systems to specialise in those crop systems best suited to their location and/or environments. Our present exploitation of recreational resources is exactly comparable with the mode of the shifting cultivation of the slash-burn-cultivate-abandon communities—worse, in fact, since our exploitation is far from being of equitable benefit to all members of our society. It is surely desirable to use transport networks and planning techniques to move away from this primitive type of recreational economy. However repugnant or expensive planning may be, the alternatives—the Exeter bypass, the approach to London from Canterbury at dusk on a summer Sunday, unplanned caravan sites on the Cornish coast or in remote Pennine dales, soaring costs of rural property, continuing conflicts between farmers and trippers—are more so.[5]

THE RURAL SETTING

The recent demographic history of rural Britain is well known,[6] but some salient points may be emphasised here. Both communication networks and industrial development have encouraged the outward movement of rural populations to urban centres. At the same time, increased mobility and prosperity has enabled workers in towns to live at increasing distances from their work, often in rural surroundings and to travel into the country at weekends. Thus not all rural areas are losing population. They may be divided into peri-urban and remote zones. The latter generally coincide with those areas which are agriculturally least productive, whilst the peri-urban zones are often in relatively fertile areas and in advantageous locations. In the remote areas the major problem is of underemployment of land, in the peri-urban areas it is one of increasing competition for land. In the former areas supplementary forms of income to agriculture are needed, in the latter some form of protection for agricultural land is necessary. Whilst recreational demands only add to the congestion in peri-urban areas, some believe that they 'offer a major, if not the major, economic opportunity for revitalisation of certain (remote) rural areas'.[7]

Rural depopulation in Britain has been most marked in two categories of employment: those of the agricultural labourer and of rural crafts/industries/services. The farming population of Britain has declined at a slower rate than that of overall depopulation. An important by-product of this differential depopulation has been that many English villages have declined in importance more than the surrounding rural areas they formerly served.

Agricultural productivity in Britain is amongst the highest in the world and has risen more rapidly in recent decades than that in almost any other sector of the economy.[8] It is essential that this productivity is not unduly impaired especially on land where it can be shown that the greatest economic/social benefit accrues from agricultural use. To date, however, one of the greatest weaknesses of rural recreational planning in Britain has been the absence of coordination with agricultural activity.

THE ASSESSMENT OF DEMAND, PRESENT AND FUTURE

At the outset it must be stated that demand for different types of recreation is impossible to measure directly, since present rates of activity are a reflection not only of demand but also of supply. Because facilities do not exist there is often no apparent demand, but the provision of the former may lead to a vigorous expansion of the latter.[9] Further, regional variations in supply apparently result in the substitution of demand for one specific activity for which facilities are lacking by other activities more readily enjoyed.[10] What follows, therefore, is a brief analysis of some of the factors which seem important, rather than either a résumé of all present demands or a survey of absolute demand.

It is relatively easy to assign quantitative values in some form to most recreations—by traffic censuses, club membership numbers, hotel users, visitor samples, etc. But it is extremely difficult to search for the motives behind or patterns of such activities, or to co-ordinate such measurements, or to forecast from them. Much of the data is non-comparable and many of the indices used relate to proxy variables at whose true significance we can only guess.

Unlike the United States, Britain has as yet no extensive surveys of consumer demand for recreation except for a Pilot National Recreation Survey undertaken by the British Travel Association and the University of Keele; of which two mimeographed reports have been issued.[11] This survey covered 3,167 respondents or about 0·006 per cent of the population. Its results, therefore, can hardly be considered statistically valid or practically applicable, but it provides the most comprehensive material available. Its general findings suggest, first and foremost, that Britain is a very inactive country all round. Only 7 per cent of the sample were engaged in active recreation on weekend afternoons (normal peak activity periods), and passive pursuits engaged only 14 per cent. Demands on the countryside for recreation are at present made by only 11 per cent of the sample at normal peak periods, considerable though the problems arising from this limited demand may be. There is obviously enormous potential for increased demand in the future.

What is likely to release this potential? A second general finding of this survey was that regional/individual prosperity is closely correlated with recreation of all sorts but notably with active pursuits. Further, that since active pursuits tend to exercise greater demands on land, increased income creates greater land-use problems. The wealthier regions of Britain are the Midlands, Metropolitan London (though here the sample survey was unrepresentative) and the South and West, whilst the North, Wales and Scotland are relatively poor. The size of the survey unfortunately means that correlation of variables with rural recreation at a regional level is statistically insignificant. Many studies of demand at individual supply points (for example, at Windsor Great Park,[12] in the Yorkshire Dales,[13] the North Yorkshire Moors,[14] the Lake District,[15] the New Forest,[16] and the Peak District,[17]) tend, however, to support the thesis that participation increases with income and car ownership ratios. The abovementioned supply-point surveys are only a sample of literally hundreds of similar surveys. As in the United States 'there has been excessive emphasis on resources-based activities', whilst in recreational demand, whether actual or latent, an important rôle *is* played by 'user-oriented forms of recreation'.[18]

Some of the evidence of these surveys is contradictory: whilst Colenutt[19] suggests that trip behaviour does not vary by socioeconomic indices, Jackson[20] found the opposite—that higher socioeconomic categories were most commonly found at relatively unpopular spots. These surveys do agree generally on important points: that visitors have travelled relatively short distances, that visitors congregate at only a few places within a recreational area, that the vast majority of visitors arrive by car, and once arrived move very short distances away from their vehicle.[21] At Windsor Great Park on a Sunday in 1966, 84 per cent of 9,000 visitors came from within thirty miles of the interview points;[22] in the Yorkshire Dales National Park on an August Saturday in 1967 a 10 per cent sample of 20,000 visitors showed that 84 per cent lived within two hours' driving distance (up to seventy miles);[23] in 1969, 91 per cent of visitors to the Lake District came from within seventy-five miles' distance.[24]

Most rural recreational areas, whatever their administrative status, seem to act in either local or regional capacities, and their main source of use is the day tripper. However, as remoteness from major population clusters increases a wider regional, and occasionally a truly national, clientele is catered for, especially in rural areas close to popular holiday coasts—Dartmoor,[25] the Pembrokeshire Coast

Table 5:1

% taking a trip to the country	Region	No. of national parks	Car * ownership	Length of * paid holiday	Income *	% families with children	% manual workers	School over 16
		y^1	y^2	y^3	y^4	y^5	y^6	y^7
10	North	5	40	169	158	41	50	19
17	Midlands	1	58	191	174	35	53	18
11	Metropolitan	0	53	170	153	36	40	29
12	South & West	2	67	166	171	39	45	30
7	Wales	3	54	170	153	39	61	17
9	Scotland	*	37	172	152	42	45	19
	Correlation Coefficients	+0·08	+0·45	+0·01	+0·58	−0·61	−0·11	+0·10

Source: Adapted from PNRS Report No. 2.

* Indices

National Park,[26] parts of Snowdonia, and, probably, Exmoor—
where seasonal concentrations of national population exist.

The general tendency of attendance at rural recreational supply
points in Britain may well fit Clawson's exponential transport
gradient[27]—provided population density around the supply point is
taken into account. Thus visitors to the Yorkshire Dales are of the
order of 1 in every 600 of population living within thirty-five miles
of the Park, 1 in 1,000 at 35–70 miles, and 1 in 2,100 at 70–105 miles.
A further factor restricting the range of influence of recreational
areas as far as day trips are concerned is that circuits are more common than straight line routes. Colenutt stated that therefore 'distance
is not a simple disutility'[28] but this mode of circuitous travel necessarily restricts the areal influence of any supply point.

If we invert this relationship it is clear that most rural recreation
at present is concentrated within a 50–70-mile radius of population
clusters. Further, the exponential transport gradient relationship
suggests that any increase in accessibility would increase attendance
in a correspondingly exponential manner. Thus Mansfield forecast
for the Lake District that a 10 per cent reduction in travel costs
brought about by road improvements would lead to a 20 per cent
increase in the number of visitors from within fifty miles and an increase of more than 30 per cent in visitors from beyond seventy miles'
distance.[29] For each recreational area, the exponent itself will differ,
according to relative attractiveness, intervening opportunities and so on.

If we know the present transport gradient, we can then have some
idea of the effect of a given road improvement. The development of
motorways is one such improvement in Britain today.[30]

Taking the figures for the Yorkshire Dales and applying to them
the present rates of attraction we may then forecast, as in Table 5:2,
likely future attendances.

Table 5:2

Time zone (hrs.)	Summer Saturday attendance 1967	Population of zones pre- motorway (m.)	Rate of attendance 1967	Population of zones* post- motorway (m.)	Future attendance
0–1	7,300	4·3	1:589	4·7	7,980
1–2	9,460	9·4	1:983	9·7	9,865
2–3	1,620	3·4	1:2099	8·2	3,910
	18,380	17·1		22·6	21,755
		Increase 18·3%			

* Assuming that all other factors remain unchanged.

The increase forecast, however, is the function of a simplified increase of only one of the variables (accessibility) involved in recreation. Actual increases will be a cumulative function of many interacting variables.

The BTA/Keele survey showed that 'possession of a car is perhaps the greatest of all stimuli to activeness in outdoor recreation',[31] although at a regional level Wales was shown to be anomalous in this respect. At present, levels of car ownership by region in Britain vary considerably but all are rising.

Table 5:3

Car ownership Levels
(cars per 100 households; 1960 = 100)

	1964[1]	1966[2]	1970 (est.)	1975 (est.)
North	39·2	42·4	49·9	61·0
Midlands	55·1	55·6	61·0	65·0
Metropolitan	55·6	55·6	59·0	63·0
South & West	63·7	64·0	67·0	70·0
Wales	50·1	53·5	59·5	64·0
Scotland	38·9	40·0	44·0	52·0
NATIONAL INDEX[2]	148	176	220	280

Sources:
[1] BTA/Keele Survey. op. cit.
[2] Burton (1967). op. cit.

If the present relationship between car ownership rates and trips to the countryside held true for the North up to 1975 then a 61 per cent car ownership rate would suggest an increase in numbers taking country trips from 10 per cent of the total population in 1967 to 15 per cent in 1975. Again, this increase would be working in isolation; in coordination, the effect of increases in all the variables positively correlated with rural recreational demand would be much greater than such individual effects.

The estimates quoted above should not be regarded as reliable: the basis for their calculation is not itself sufficiently detailed. Nevertheless they do indicate likely trends; trends that expand demand at a geometrical rate. The potential demand for countryside recreation will indeed be revealed and realised at increasingly rapid rates.

New types of demand are likely to arise in the future. Analysis of present trends within Britain will be of little value in forecasting their significance. Of such types, one of the more problematical is likely to be that of the second house or country cottage. There has already been enormous growth in this field, but, apart from work in progress at Wye College, little has been written on the subject in Britain. In Europe, the story is different. In 1963, 25 per cent of all Swedish holiday-makers spent their vacation in their own summer houses.[32] In 1965 there were 300,000 such second houses and by 1971 there may be 550,000.[33] In Denmark there were 130,000 such residences in 1967.[34] In France 16·4 per cent of a sampled population in Lille possessed second houses in 1964.[35] Many such homes are located in coastal areas: on the Île de Ré, Madame Bordarier describes how in some villages over half the homes are owned by Parisians[36] whilst second homes are now the most common feature on the Channel coast.[37] In addition, however, such residences are common throughout rural France.[38] In Norway, towns are 'virtually dead from Saturday lunchtime onwards, people being at their weekend cottages or out on a ramble' (on foot or on skis).[39]

Few if any British holidays are *recorded* as being spent in second homes,[40] whilst the BTA/Keele survey sample contained only 2 per cent who owned such properties. It may well be that caravans are the British substitute. Nevertheless in many areas pressure for such homes already exists; in the Yorkshire Dales some hamlets and villages (Reeth, Kettlewell, Horsehouse and Dent) have from 20–50 per cent of their homes so occupied. These houses are readily recognised as in France: *'les maisons amenagées des citadins se remarquent par leur entretien et leur aspect coquet au milieu d'habitations restées rustiques ou frappées d'abandon'.*[41]

Problems of such properties mentioned by foreign writers are already apparent in Britain. In France, David[42] claims that the second residence is precipitating agricultural decline and the exodus of rural population by pricing agriculture and farmers out of the land market. In Norway, when access to remote areas is improved 'the first vehicle down the new road is a removal lorry; the first up is, perhaps, the lorry carrying materials for the first "hytte" '. A few wealthy townsfolk buy up cheaply large areas of farmland and proceed to exclude their fellow citizens, being most vocal in objecting to rural development, and occasionally to make very high profit margins on 'hytte' development.[43]

In Britain strict planning for landscape conservation has meant that only those town-dwellers able to afford the special paints, local stone and tiles and architectural advice have been able to move into select rural areas. Worse, the price of existing housing in the Yorkshire Dales, having risen by six to twelve times in twenty years, now

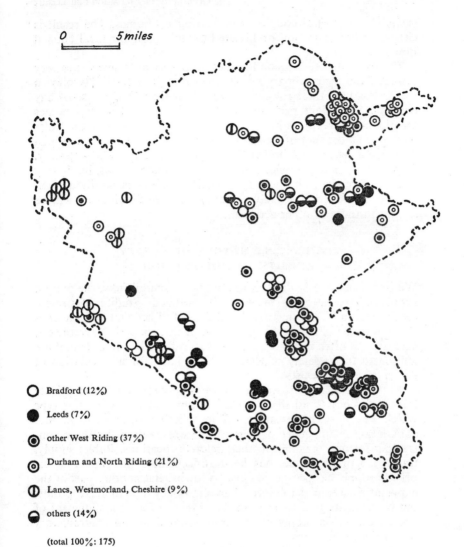

O   Bradford (12%)

●   Leeds (7%)

◉   other West Riding (37%)

◎   Durham and North Riding (21%)

◑   Lancs, Westmorland, Cheshire (9%)

◒   others (14%)

(total 100%: 175)

Fig. 3

Origins of newcomers to the Yorkshire Dales
(note: this map is not comprehensive)
Source: Planning Registers

exclude young rural couples from setting up homes. The result is either further migration or higher building costs for local council housing.

The owners of such second homes do not seem to select sites very distant from their primary homes even though accessibility plays a rather less important rôle in site selection than in the case of day trippers. Sixty-eight per cent of the Lillois-owned second homes mentioned above lay within sixty miles of the city, whilst in the Dales well over 80 per cent of second homes shown in Figure 3 are owned by persons whose first homes lie less than three hours' drive away. This may be merely a reflection of present work patterns, but it may also indicate that, although the second home is primarily a high-income investment, its likely pattern of future distribution will be similar to those of other activities.

THE PRESENT NATURE OF SUPPLY
AND ITS ADMINISTRATION

Whilst it is extremely difficult to analyse 'demand' fully, the present supply of recreation is more easily outlined. Studies of present supply are, in fact, numerous[44] and for a full account the reader is referred to the bibliography at the end of this chapter. Nevertheless, such studies often relate to present use—rather than to potential use and/or to the capacity of use: 'no firm basis for a calculation of carrying capacity exists'.[45]

At present there exist strong contrasts between public and private forms of supply; and there is little doubt that it is the latter type which has been more successful in meeting open demand and stimulating latent demand. Part of the explanation for these contrasting fortunes has lain in their relative locations. Public supply, up to the present time, has been concentrated in remoter areas, private supply has prospered close to towns. But another part of the explanation lies in the failure of public policy, not to make profits, but to define its goals clearly. In the absence of such a statement of objectives, public supply has been dominated by self contradictory or restrictive decisions.

It has been generally agreed that two conflicting strands of thought have dominated British recreational planning—conservation and use.[46] The early success of Canon Rawnsley and the National Trust in preserving small areas of land of generally acknowledged beauty inspired later planners in the idea of preservation of 'natural beauty' as a basic tenet of rural planning. John Dower, the architect of Britain's National Parks,[47] clearly had this in mind when he suggested the following four basic planning functions in 'extensive areas of beautiful and relatively wild country':

(1) the characteristic landscape should be strictly preserved,
(2) access and facilities for public open-air enjoyment should be amply provided,
(3) wild life and buildings and places of architectural and historical interest should be suitably protected, whilst
(4) established farming use should be effectively maintained.

The recreational function of these areas was to be biased strongly towards walkers and ramblers, cyclists were to be tolerated,[48] but little or no consideration was given to mass motorised recreation.

The National Parks and Access to the Countryside Act of 1949[49] set up the machinery and administration whereby National Parks, Areas of Outstanding National Beauty and other facilities could be established under the National Parks Commission.[50] The functions of this body were first to preserve and enhance 'natural beauty', and second, to promote the enjoyment of the specified areas by the public. No suggestion was made as to how the seemingly basic conflict between conservation and use was to be overcome, nor was mention made of the difficulty of planning alongside rapidly changing agriculture. Most important, the Act did not specify adequately either the administration or the financial provisions available for this difficult task.

To generalise, the result was that the National Parks Commission had an unhappy existence. The emphasis on preservation was most easily accomplished by restrictive planning, which antagonised rural populations within the specified areas and frustrated recreational demand without preventing its unplanned expression. The expenditure on the Parks was pitifully small—'one-tenth of the old London County Council's expenditure on its Parks Service'[51]—and constructive planning of recreational facilities was neglected. Some of the administrative arrangements made were ludicrous: the two principal objectors to the establishment of the Yorkshire Dales National Park were the West and North Ridings County Councils, between whose territories the Park was divided, yet when the Park was established the Minister of Housing and Local Government ordered that its administration should be placed in the hands of these Councils, its greatest opponents.

But beyond the Act lay a second reason for the failures of the National Parks Commission: all the National Parks lay north-west of the Humber–Exe line. This meant, first, that 40 per cent of the population of England and Wales lived more than fifty miles from any Park, whilst some areas (south-east Lancashire, west Yorkshire) had at least three Parks within that distance. Secondly, it meant that the Parks were established in those areas least able to take advantage of their benefits, as seen previously. Thirdly, the Parks were located in areas least able to finance them. The Parks fell under County Council control whilst their users, town-dwellers, lived for the most part in County Boroughs. Hence the burden of payment for Parks fell, amongst others, on the rural populations themselves.

Concepts of National Parks vary widely throughout the world. Outside Europe they are generally regarded as *sancti sanctorum*,[52] the last bastions of nature. Most countries in Europe have faced those problems mentioned in connection with Britain. Their basic solution seems to have lain generally with land use specialisation. 'Territorial separation of science and tourism is insisted upon' in Poland[53] where the Parks, admittedly largely of forest, consist of an accessible periphery surrounding a core of limited access. Likewise in Czechoslovakia the High Tatras National Park[54] has been separated into concentric zones: an inner, strictly preserved area; an intermediary zone where grazing is forbidden; and an outer zone of land use. In France also concentric zoning has been introduced, with the variation that tourist development is encouraged on the peripheries of the Parks.[55]

It can be argued that in Britain we are conserving landscapes rather than flora or fauna, and hence the above remarks do not apply. However, we must accept that because the Parks 'are not natural landscapes' but 'harmonised landscapes reflecting centuries of historical evolution'[56] under man's hands then these landscapes must change. If we wish to *preserve* such landscapes, or portions of them, then the Danish and German practice of public compensation for farmers in preservation zones may be the only practical solution.[57]

In the past five years, attitudes amongst planners towards rural recreation have swung sharply in favour of recreation rather than preservation.[58] In the Countryside Act[59] the main purpose 'is to provide for the improvement of facilities for the enjoyment of the countryside by the public. . . .' This Act also partly corrects some of the financial mistakes of its predecessor. It is to be hoped, however, that the new Act will not abandon preservation. The view expressed here is that there is rarely conflict between use and preservation when National Parks are looked at in detail and that there is some danger that the new vogue is merely a reaction against previous failures which itself will end in failure. However, the Act also ushers in an important new aspect to rural recreation. In the spectrum of recreational facilities, the greatest gap in British planning lay in the peri-urban areas and the provision of regional recreational facilities.[60] Some of these gaps had been filled by private entrepreneurs (Woburn Abbey for example) or enterprising local councils.[61]

One of the most useful concepts available to administrators of recreational areas is that of carrying capacity. Obviously the capacity will vary according to the specified need, so that each resource will have a whole series of capacity assessments. The decision to utilise one assessment rather than any other will depend upon the specific demand made on the area (if already in use), or planning decisions on desirable future use. The technique was used in planning the tourist industry of Donegal (see p. 62, where the criticisms refer not to the technique but to its particular implementation). Dower gives striking examples of its use in the United States.[62] Once an assessment is decided upon, capacity can be controlled by the volume of facilities provided. For instance, Rice[63] showed that since most visitors come to the North Yorkshire Moors by car, then attendance at any particular attraction is controlled by the amount of car parking available in these areas. Similar arrangements have been relatively successful in the Bolton Abbey and Malham areas of the Yorkshire Dales.

THE ALLOCATION OF RESOURCES

Demand is variable both in time (changes in type) and space (regional variations). It is also flexible insofar as it can be deflected or created. In general it will continue to expand. Supply of rural recreation is also variable and can be improved by the provision of facilities. In the long run, however, supply is finite, and even in the short run, since additional facilities are expensive, it is a scarce resource. It seems clear, therefore, that the burden of planning rural recreation does lie with the allocation of scarce resources even if a basic consideration should be the source of demand.

Those activities laying claim to these rural resources have to be established by society as a whole and some order of priority must be assigned to each such activity. In this chapter, demand for recreation has been given special treatment, but other activities do seem to be considered important by society. Amongst these are agriculture, whose progress should not be impeded unduly, and the preservation of sites of scientific and cultural interest. Since the last named cannot be increased by additional investment (except, perhaps, in the case of archaeology) it would seem logical that, once accepted as having a valid claim on rural resources, they should receive strict priority.

D*

There is a strong case for suggesting that whilst rural recreation is at present predominantly a regional and local activity, agriculture and site preservation are national ones. It is also clear that regional claims should always give way to national interests. It must then follow that recreational activities at a regional level must give precedence, first, to site preservation and, second, to national agricultural requirements.

Site preservation is obviously based on very specific resources. Although location plays a rôle in agriculture, specific soil and climatic resources still dominate its demands. In regional recreation location is a dominant factor and because of this recreational resources are much more expandable. Although these priorities will remain relatively standard their absolute claims in any one area will differ. A specific case, therefore—the present Yorkshire Dales National Park—will be taken to illustrate the general assumptions and principles for rural resources allocations made here.

THE YORKSHIRE DALES NATIONAL PARK—AN EXAMPLE

(1) *Preservation*

Geologically, the Yorkshire Dales are unique in England for their karst scenery. At present many individual features (Alum Pot, Goredale Scar) are declared Sites of Special Scientific Interest. There is a case for the designation of the whole of the limestone block as an area of landscape preservation. The area is largely inaccessible at present, save on foot, and its agricultural value is generally low. It should be noted that, at present, many SSSIs are not strictly preserved but are subject to intense use—in some cases, use of specialists, such as potholers, whilst many others which could be designated SSSI are popular as picnic sites—Hardraw Force, Aysgarth Falls and the Strid. Whilst facilities at these latter sites for recreation could be readily improved, others could just as readily be more strictly preserved for their 'natural' setting or ecological value— Whitefield Gill Force in Wensleydale or lower Kisdon Force in Swaledale. It is notable that all the falls visited at present are close to road access points. The tendency of visitors to congregate at beauty spots where facilities are readily available and to shun those places where access is more difficult and facilities absent is useful for the planner. A third major set of geological features worth both development *and* preservation (for educational and scientific purposes) are the old mining areas. Some parts of these defunct mining zones are accessible, others lie in remote valleys. Mining museums and reconstructed lead mills at Grassington and Reeth

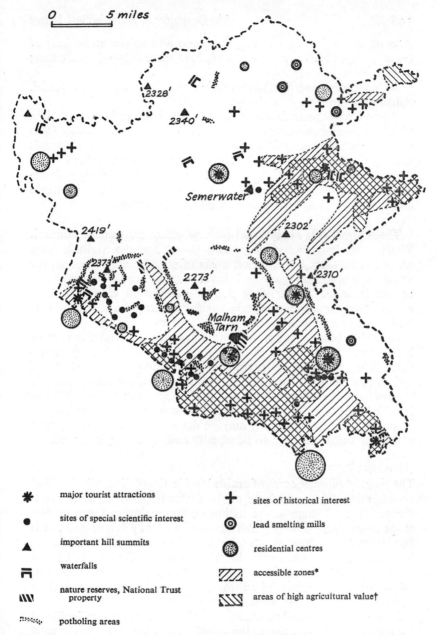

	major tourist attractions		sites of historical interest
●	sites of special scientific interest	◎	lead smelting mills
▲	important hill summits		residential centres
	waterfalls		accessible zones*
	nature reserves, National Trust property		areas of high agricultural value†
	potholing areas		

* Simplified from a series of maps in Jackson (1966) op. cit., showing accessibility patterns from North Lancashire, the West Riding and Durham. The areas shown here are those to which the total travelling time from Burnley, Leeds and Darlington is less than 300 minutes.

† Areas in which livestock units per acre are greater than the national average.

Fig. 4

Present recreational use of the Yorkshire Dales National Park (two of the major tourist villages) would add to the attractions of these 'honeypots'. The assumptions behind these suggestions are that:

(a) educational recreation can be just as enjoyable, if not more so, than hours in bric-à-brac shops;

(b) to invest many facilities in one or two accessible points is a viable means of concentrating many forms of demand (away from areas in which preservation is being encouraged) and economic activity (in the revitalisation of rural communities); and that

(c) if preservation is to be successful it should be strictly enforceable; restrictions however intrinsically reasonable are more palatable if they are matched by improved facilities elsewhere.

These arguments apply to all sites, whether physical or cultural. Whilst Colt Park Wood, Cam Gill Wood and the Malham Tarn areas can be literally fenced off areas of strictly limited access, the woodlands at Grassington and Aysgarth Falls could be developed as picnic areas. The guiding factor involved in choice between preservation or development is basically that of assessibility—its limitation or its enhancement.

A further basic assumption in this argument is that the conflict between preservation and use is not total and, indeed, is fairly superficial. A single orchid, perhaps, cannot be studied by botanists *and* picked by a picnicker from Bradford. But most of our rural resources are not so limited—we have *areas* of landscapes, several waterfalls and hundreds of examples of traditional architecture, some of which may be preserved, some of which may be developed. Both development and preservation do need to be equally and effectively enforced.

(2) *Agriculture*

There are hardly five acres of arable land in the National Park of 680 square miles. The agriculture of the Dales is pastoral. If we assess the agricultural value to the nation of this region in terms of livestock alone, only a very small portion is of any importance. It is fair to say then that agricultural activity in the Dales, considered in isolation, does not have overwhelming claims on the nation. In view of this, and of the nature of landscape taste, the use of some parts of the area for commercial afforestation combined with some form of recreation would not seem inappropriate.

Nevertheless in detail the claims of agriculture are not insignificant for they are most intensive in the valley areas which are also the most accessible areas for recreationists. In these areas it should not be impossible to combine agriculture with recreation. The major tourist attractions are water, woodland, villages and their facilities and other miscellaneous attractions such as disused mines. Of these, few really conflict with the farmers' need for good hay/pasture land. Further, in the accessible areas farmers should be encouraged to participate in the tourist trade although the details of development would require planning control.

(3) *Recreation*

On a normal summer weekend more than 20,000 car-borne visitors come to the Dales. In addition 2,500 come by coach, up to 550 young cyclists and hill-walkers spend Saturday nights in Youth Hostels, another 400 people may spend the night in hotels and guest houses, about 400 potholers and climbers will camp, 2,500 people will live in their caravans and well over 1,000 will stay in their own second homes. As will be seen, by far the greatest number of visitors are motorists.

Paradoxically the minor activities create most of the problems. Firstly because the majority who depend on road access are restricted to relatively small areas of the Park and tend to congregate at a few places along an even fewer number of popular routes. Secondly— because the details of the road network show that most popular valleys could, without very much extension of their existing roads, adopt a one-way traffic system at weekends to absorb increased traffic if necessary. The less numerically significant but more active pursuits in many ways have more widespread effects and already show signs of overusing existing resources. As in the Lake District and Snowdonia, climbers often have to queue more often than traffic, and likewise potholers are beginning to find popular caves overcrowded. In these activities and in others such as fishing, camping, walking and possibly sailing, many organisations would welcome a more unified form of supervision to ensure fair allotment of facilities. It is suggested that for these specialised activities which often take place in remoter areas rationed resource allocation is becoming inevitable. At the same time facilities for these activities are usually non-existent. If facilities, such as training centres or simple accommodation, are provided through public funds then their users should also be expected to pay for the use of them.

Rural recreation, however considerable it is at the moment, touches only a relatively small section of the potential demand. This demand will be realised by the growth of mobility but may be moulded by selective accessibility and facility provision. In assessing claims for resource allocation matters of national interest such as site preser-

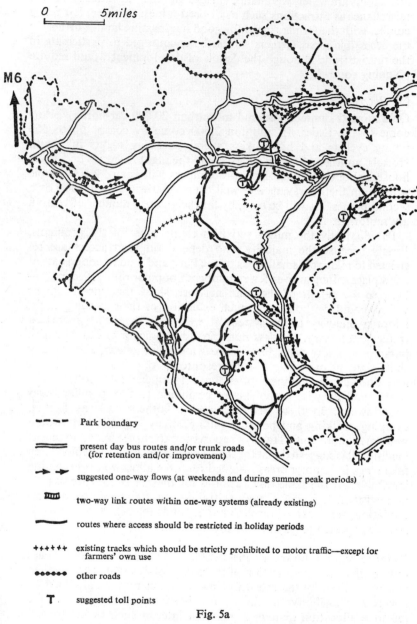

0   5miles

M6

- − − − Park boundary

━━━━ present day bus routes and/or trunk roads
(for retention and/or improvement)

━▶ ━ ▶ suggested one-way flows (at weekends and during summer peak periods)

▥▥▥ two-way link routes within one-way systems (already existing)

━━━ routes where access should be restricted in holiday periods

+ + + + + + existing tracks which should be strictly prohibited to motor traffic—except for
farmers' own use

●●●●●● other roads

T suggested toll points

Fig. 5a

Suggested transport networks in the Yorkshire Dales

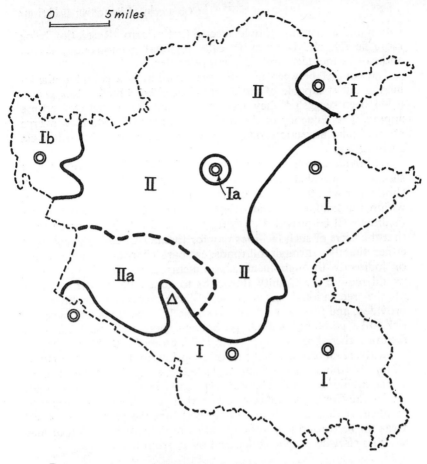

I   area in which present demand is already great

Ia   Hawes, an island of development which should partake in amenity development. It is important that this should not apply, however, to Wensleydale as a whole

Ib   Sedbergh and the Howgill Fells. A little used area at present but one in which increasing pressure is being brought about by the M6

II   area in which development should be strictly forbidden; in which the toll road could play a useful part; in which farmers should receive special 'landscape' subsidies; in which preservation is the rule

IIa   notwithstanding the above, 11a is demonstrated as an area of organised mountain sports. Development should be concentrated at the suggested centre at Horton

◎   centres for amenity development

△   suggested centre at Horton

Fig. 5b

Suggested land-use zones in the Yorkshire Dales

vation and agriculture should receive first priority. Recreation being more flexible and being a basically regional phenomenon, should and can be moulded around these priorities.

The conflict between use and preservation is a complex phenomenon but is capable of settlement. For either function to succeed, it has been suggested, they need to be strictly separated by land-use zoning. The tendency of the majority of recreationists to converge on particular attractions or use only certain scenic routes will assist such zoning.

Within recreational areas many more facilities than at present exist should be provided. Wherever possible, the local rural population should participate in the economic benefits accruing from recreation, within the confines of the overall strategy. However, since many facilities will be provided out of public funds, it should be ensured that the users of such facilities pay for them. This could be achieved either directly—through toll roads, car park charges, entrance fees— or indirectly through local government rates. The latter course would require the County Boroughs to contribute to the expenses of the recreational programme. Where specialist facilities are provided, and for many activities especially those involving personal risk—like climbing, sailing, potholing—there is a need for such facilities, then direct charges seem to be more acceptable.

Lastly, rural recreation is part of a continuum. In the past portions of this continuum have been neglected (just as they have received scarce attention in this chapter) especially in the peri-urban areas. Under the Countryside Act it is hoped that such gaps will begin to be filled. If that is so then we may find that the pressures on rural areas for recreation will not expand as rapidly, as provision of new facilities elsewhere siphons demand away from them.

1. Cullingworth, J. B., 1964. Planning for leisure, *Urban Studies*, p. 1; for a Soviet view see: Gerasimov, I. P. *et al.*, 1970. Current geographical problems in recreational planning, *Soviet Geography*, p. 189.
2. Rodgers, H. B., 1969. Leisure and recreation, *Urban Studies*, p. 368.
3. British Travel Association (BTA)/University of Keele, 1967/9. *Pilot National Recreation Survey Reports*, 1 & 2.
4. Rodgers. op. cit.
5. See, for example, Norton, G. A., 1970. Public outdoor recreation and resource allocation: a welfare approach, *Land Economics* XLVI, p. 414.
6. Lawton, R., 1967. Depopulation in Nineteenth Century England, *Liverpool Essays in Geography* (Eds. Steel, R. W., and Lawton, R.).
7. Harper, R. A., Schmudde, T. H., and Thomas, F. H., 1966. Recreation based economic development and the growth point concept, *Land Economics*,

p. 95; Burton, T. L., 1967. *Outdoor Recreational Enterprises in Problem Rural Areas.* Wye College, London.
8. McCrone, G., 1963. *Agricultural Integration in Western Europe,* PEP, no. 470.
9. BTA/University of Keele. op. cit.
10. ibid.
11. ibid.
12. Burton, T. L., 1967. *Windsor Great Park: A Recreational Survey.* Wye College, London.
13. North Riding/West Riding County Councils, 1966. *Traffic in the Yorkshire Dales National Park;* Jackson, R. T., 1966. *The Yorkshire Dales as a National Park.* Unpublished D.Phil. thesis, University of Oxford.
14. Rice, W. F., 1966. *Recreational Landscapes in the Region of the North Yorkshire Moors National Park.* Unpublished M.A. thesis, University of London.
15. Dunmur, J. V., 1967. *Conservation and Planning in the Lake District National Park.* Unpublished B.Litt. thesis, University of Oxford.
16. Millar, L., 1967. *A Study of the Longterm Problems of Traffic and Accessibility in Rural areas of High Amenity Value with special reference to the New Forest.* Unpublished M.Sc. thesis, University of Southampton.
17. BTA, 1965. *Survey of the Peak District National Park.*
18. Wolfe, R. I., 1964. Perspective on outdoor recreation, *Geog. Rev.,* p. 203.
19. Colenutt, R. J., 1969. Modelling traffic patterns of day visitors to the countryside, *Area,* no. 2, p. 43.
20. Jackson, R. T., 1968. *Surveys of Visitors to the Yorkshire Dales.* Unpublished ms.
21. Burton, T. L., and Wibberley, G. P., 1965. *Outdoor Recreation in the British Countryside.* Wye College, London; Wager, J., 1965. Outdoor recreation on common-land, *Jnl. Town Plan. Inst.*
22. Burton, 1967b. op. cit.
23. Jackson, 1968. op. cit.
24. Yapp, W. B., 1969. *The Weekend Motorist in the Lake District National Park.* Cyclostyled copy in Countryside Commission Library; Lake District Planning Board, 1965. *Report on Traffic in the Lake District National Park.*
25. Board, C., *et al.,* 1970. People on Dartmoor, *Geog. Mag.,* p. 266.
26. Barrett, J. N., 1970. Progress on a coastal path, *Geog. Mag.,* p. 292.
27. Clawson, M., 1959. *Methods for measuring the demand for and value of outdoor recreation.* Washington DC, Resources for the future.
28. Colenutt. op. cit.
29. Mansfield, N. W., 1969. Recreational trip generation, *Jnl. Trans. & Econ. Policy,* p. 152.
30. Jackson, R. T., 1970. Motorways and National Parks in Britain, *Area,* no. 4, p. 26; Cracknell, B., 1967. Access to the countryside, *Regional Studies,* p. 147; Ellis, J. B., and Van Doren, C. S., 1966. A comparative evaluation of gravity and systems theory models for statewide recreational traffic flow, *Jnl. Reg. Sci.,* p. 57; Crevo, C. C., 1963. Characteristics of summer weekend recreational travel, *Highway Research Record,* p. 51.
31. BTA/University of Keele. op. cit.
32. Burton, T. L., 1966. Outdoor recreation in America, Sweden and Britain, *Town and Country Planning,* p. 456.
33. Palme, O., 1966. Time on one's hands, *Progress,* p. 113; Tobe, E., 1968. Planning for leisure in Sweden, *Proc. XIIth Int. Cong. of Surveyors.*
34. Boe, E., 1968. Planning for leisure in Denmark, *Proc. XIIth Int. Cong. of Surveyors.*

114 The Geography of Recreation and Leisure

35. Dacquin, J.-P., 1965. Les residences secondaires des Lillois, *Hommes et Terres du Nord*, p. 48.
36. Bordarier, M., 1966. Le tourisme dans l'Île de Ré, *Norois*, p. 453.
37. Cribier, F., 1965. Les estivants au Touquet, *Ann. de Géog.*, p. 38.
38. Marie, R., 1966. Quelques traits d'évolution de l'activité touristique, *Rev. Géog. Alp.*, p. 177.
39. Somme, K., *et. al.*, 1966. *Fjellbygd of Ferrefjell*. Oslo.
40. Burton, 1966. op. cit.
41. Wolokowitsch, M., 1963. Recherches sur le tourisme, *Méditérranée*, p. 67.
42. David, J., 1966. Residences secondaires et structures fonçières dans le Val du Bourget, *Rev. Geog. Alp.*, p. 489.
43. Somme, *et al.* op. cit.
44. Coppock, J. T., 1966. The recreational use of land and water in rural Britain, *Tidjs. Econ. soc. geog.*, p. 81; Patmore, J. A., 1970. *Land and Leisure*. Newton Abbot; Weir, T., 1967. The Scottish countryside in 1967. *Town and Country Planning*, p. 309.
45. Rodgers, 1969. op. cit.
46. For a good review of the background to the legislation see Blenkinsop, A., 1964. The National Parks of England and Wales, *Planning Outlook*, p. 9; Beltran, E., 1962. Use and conservation: Two conflicting principles, *Proc. 1st World Conf. on Nat. Parks*. Washington.
47. Dower, J., 1945. *National Parks in England and Wales*. HMSO Cmnd. 6628.
48. See a series of articles by Dower, John, published in *The Dalesman* (Clapham, Yorkshire) in 1942.
49. *National Parks and Access to the Countryside Act 1949*, 12, 13 and 14 Geo. VI, ch. 97.
50. Blenkinsop. op. cit.
51. Conservative Political Centre, 1966. *A Better Country*.
52. Badshah, M. A., and Bhadran, C. A. R., 1962. National Parks: their principles and purpose. *Proc. 1st World Conf. on Nat. Parks*. Washington.
53. Szczesny, T., 1967. La contribution de l'architecte paysagiste a l'amenagement des Parcs Nationaux, *Pap. & Proc. IUCN*, p. 8.
54. Simmons, I. G., 1968. *The Conservation of Nature and Landscape, and the Development of Outdoor Recreation Reserves in the Czechoslovak SSR*. Mimeographed paper in the Countryside Commission Library.
55. The French Embassy, London, 1967. *Nature Conservation in France*.
56. Staffordshire County Council, n.d. *Planning for Recreation*.
57. Deutscher Rat fur Landespflege, 1967. *Guiding Principles for Legal Steps Concerning Landscape Preservation*. Bonn.
58. Hookway, R. J. S., 1968. Planning for Leisure and Recreation, *Proc. XXIInd Oxford Farmers Conf.*, p. 44; Hookway, R. J. S., 1968. *Investment in Recreation*. Paper read at the National Parks Annual Conference.
59. Furmidge, J., 1969. Planning for recreation in the countryside, *Jnl. Town Plan. Inst.*, p. 63.
60. Masser, I., 1966. The use of outdoor recreation facilities, *Town Plan. Rev.*, p. 41; Executive Committee of the Town and Country Planning Association, 1965. A policy for countryside recreation in England and Wales, *Town and Country Plan*, p. 473.
61. Wibberley, G. P., 1968. Pressures on Britain's rural land, *Proc. XXIInd Oxford Farmers Conf.*, p. 1; see for example: Rugby Joint Water Board, 1969. *The Use of Draycote and Stanford Reservoirs for Recreation*; Colne Valley Working Party, 1967. *Studies for a Regional Park*. Hillingdon; Huxley, T., and Pratt, J., 1966. *Preliminary Survey of Holyrood Park*;

Lovett, W. B., 1962. Leisure and land use in the metropolitan Green Belt, *Jnl. Town Plan. Inst.*, p. 150.
62. Dower, M., 1970. Leisure—its impact on man and the land, *Geography*, p. 253; Dower, M., and McCarthy, P. E., 1967. Planning for conservation and development, *Jnl. Town Plan. Inst.*, p. 99. Taylor, G. D., 1955. An approach to the inventory of recreation, *Canad. Geog.*, p. 84.
63. Rice. op. cit.

6

PLANNING FOR THE RECREATIONAL USE OF

THE COASTS OF BRITAIN

The problems which face planners of the British countryside include the complexity of the distribution of its recreational resources. Along the coasts of Britain, however, the resources which attract visitors are much more clearly defined: although not continuous they are zonal. In the past, the demand for such leisure resources has been sufficiently small and the means of exploitation (the railway) insufficiently flexible to allow more than a piecemeal development of the coast. The past twenty years have seen a rapid increase in demand and the widespread use of the more flexible motor-car. On the coast of Britain the spatial consequences of these demands has been more clearly expressed than anywhere else largely because of the clearly defined nature of the resource, whilst the story of the seaside resort since 1945 has been a model of British urban development in general, although exhibiting peculiar features of its own.

The results of both growing demand and growing flexibility of expression of demand have been: the spread of holiday activities to almost the whole of the accessible shore-line; the development of more and more specialised forms of recreation which have special environmental requirements; the reaction of conservation interests; and the changed function of the nucleated resort town notably towards industrialisation and residential retirement.

THE HOLIDAY AREAS

A cursory glance at Table 6:1 suggests that there has been a growth in national as opposed to regional resort areas in recent years. That

is whilst some areas, especially the South West and Wales, have
increased their share of the holiday trade, others, notably the South
East and the North/North East have declined. The measure of

Table 6:1

Distribution of British holidays according to regions

Region	1951 (%)	1962 (%)	1968 (%)
South West	14	19	22
South	12	13	16
Wales	9	10	13
Scotland	10	10	11
North West	11	12	11
South East	13	12	10
East	8	10	8
North/North East	10	10	8
Midlands	6	6	7
London/Middlesex	7	4	3
TOTALS (m.)	25	32	30
STANDARD DEVIATION	2·45	3·83	4·98

Source: British Travel Association, 1969. *The British on
Holiday*. Mimeo.

concentration of holidaymaking, previously weak, has increased,
and the ties between industrial regions and specific holiday resorts
have been reduced. However, two other salient points emerge from
the table. First, that touring holidays have increased whilst, second,
overall demand for holidays which increased in the 1950s was
stagnant in the following decade. The former is a simple pointer to a
major feature of post-war holiday development—the geographical
spread of holiday-making to areas previously ignored. In fact,
whilst on the one hand certain national holiday areas as noted above
have become more readily differentiated, on the other hand all
holiday areas have experienced the dispersal of this activity. The
second point raises the question of why should demand have apparently slackened?

Before attempting to answer this question, a definition of 'holiday'
would be useful. According to the British Travel Association, from
whose data Table 6:1 and much subsequent information is derived,
'the holiday is defined as four or more nights spent away from home'.
Given this, rising living standards in Britain, coupled with the
increasingly competitive position of foreign package tours *vis-à-vis*

the traditional British boarding-house holiday, have led to a rapid
rise in the number of foreign holidays taken. Thus whilst domestic
holiday expenditure has risen by 78 per cent (from £320 million in
1951 to £570 million in 1968) British tourist-spending abroad rose
from £60 million in 1951 to £320 million in 1968. Whereas in 1951
foreign holidays accounted for only 16 per cent of total expenditure
in 1968 they represented 36 per cent.[1] Foreign travel has been
especially important amongst the higher socio-economic groups and
amongst the young (see Table 6:2). In fact these two groups exert
more demand in all fields of recreation. The traditional type of
holiday has become the preserve of the poor and the old.

Table 6:2

Holiday-makers by age and socio-economic group

	% of all adults	% having no holiday	% GB holiday	% abroad holiday
(a) AGE				
16–24	17	15	18	25
25–34	16	16	16	15
35–49	26	23	28	27
50 upwards	40	47	38	33
TOTAL	100	100	100	100
(b) SOCIO-ECONOMIC GROUP				
AB	14	7	16	29
CI	22	15	26	32
C2, D & E	64	78	58	38
TOTAL	100	100	100	100

Source: BTA. op. cit.

Within Britain the demand for 'holidays' has become geographically more diffused, undermining still further the established resorts.
Ownership of a car does not necessarily lead to increased holiday-
making.[2] Even so, the importance of this means of transport for
holidays has increased rapidly (see Table 6:3). The railway, which
created the nucleated resort towns, is still important there—although rarely does it account for more than half the holiday visitors'
transport. It is especially important for old people and for those
without a car. On the whole, however, it has been replaced by the
car and many coastal railway branch lines are now closed.

Table 6:3

Transport of holiday-makers

Type	1951 (%)	1962 (%)	1968 (%)
Car	27	54	66
Bus	27	18	16
Rail	47	26	14

Source: BTA. op. cit.

Whilst the car has encouraged the development of small resort villages either through touring or residential holidays, a further element of dispersal has been added by the rising costs of the traditional holiday. The caravan site necessarily located away from existing resorts (because of land values) has become a familiar part of the annual holiday scene. During the 1950s this form of cheaper holiday grew at the expense of accommodation in friends'/relatives' homes (see Table 6:4) and more seriously in the following decade

Table 6:4

Holiday by type of accommodation

Type	1951 (%)	1962 (%)	1968 (%)
Licensed hotel	10	14	14
Unlicensed hotel	31	31	23
Friends/Relations	36	26	25
Caravans	—	13	16
Rented	8	8	9
Holiday camps	3	5	5
Camping	4	4	4
Others	15	4	6
TOTAL	107*	105	104

Source: BTA. op. cit.

* Totals more than 100 because of mixed holidays.

attracted custom away from the boarding guest house. The cost of a caravan holiday is estimated at between only 45–60 per cent of a more traditional form of accommodation.[3]

SHORT STAY VISITS TO THE COAST

By taking the definition of a holiday as a stay of four or more nights, we underestimate considerably the degree and geographical extent of the pressure on coastal land use. At the same time as foreign holidays have reduced the growth rate of domestic holidaymaking, so there has been a rapid expansion in short stay uses of the coast. Although it is difficult to specify exactly this growth, these activities fall into three main categories: the holiday cottage, the caravan, and the day trip.

The holiday cottage on the coast, like its country cousin, is utilised throughout the year over weekends and short holidays as a local base for other recreational activities. Amongst the most important of these latter is sailing. The various estimates disagree on the exact extent of this activity but all agree on its rapid growth. Between 1952 and 1962 the membership of sailing clubs increased from 13,000 to 250,000.[4] By 1966, Jessop estimated that about 700,000 people took an active interest in the sport and that this number was growing by 8 per cent per annum.[5] 'Few sports are more closely geared to income level'[6] and it may be expected that this increase will continue with increased personal wealth. Regionally the demand for this activity is strongly concentrated in South, West and in South East England, along these coasts the pressure for moorings, dinghy parks, and marinas is increasing steadily, already causing congestion. Pressure is not absent elsewhere and Jessop states that as a result the price of small cottages on the North Wales coast has risen twelve-fold since 1930.

Whilst caravan holidays have increased rapidly, the figures given in Table 6:4 do not give a realistic impression of their impact. This is partly because the caravan is even more frequently used for short stays, and, unlike the hotel or boarding house, the individual caravan is usually used by only a handful of holiday-makers, often by only one family. Over half the total accommodation in Wales is in caravan beds[7] as also in East Anglia[8] and many other places. Officially the number of Caravan Club members rose by 400 per cent 1955–64 and is now over 120,000. Actually it is estimated that there are more than ten times this number of caravan users. Over 75 per cent of caravan sites are within three miles of the coast[9] and such sites have become valuable property. Rawnsley[10] quotes an instance of land for such a site near Flamborough Head changing hands at £9,200 an acre or £380 per caravan place.

At present about twenty million people a year in Britain do not take a holiday. Of these 78 per cent (15·6 m.) are in lower income groups.[11] If these people in future are to become holiday-makers then they are likely to add to demands for caravaning especially in view of the present low cost of such holidays. However, with both increasing coastal land prices and planning restrictions the price is now rising and, unlikely though it may seem, the foreign resort may offer more attractions for lower income groups in the future. Certainly, some planning officials believe that the caravan boom is tailing off.[12]

Although the day trip, as we have seen, is the oldest form of popular coastal recreation it still retains this popularity. Towns like Brighton deal with over six and a half million day visitors a year and although the number of staying visitors at Blackpool has declined recently the number of day trips to the town is now over eight million. The day trip is the one form of short stay coastal use which is still a characteristic of the traditional holiday resort. Whilst the peak ratio between staying and day visitors at Brighton is about 1:5, along the coast of West Sussex it is only 1:1·3.[13]

From these various types of development there have arisen two major problems of coastal use. On the one hand there is the growing concern for the conservation of the coastline and the restriction of further developmental spread. On the other hand there is the complex problem of the traditional seaside resort whose importance and functions have been reduced and diversified respectively.

CONSERVATION

Approximately 27 per cent of the English coastline and 21 per cent of that of Wales is now developed as built-up areas or as industrial land. The degree of development varies from nil on the tidal marsh coast of Holland, to about 70 per cent in West Sussex (recreational and residential use) and Denbighshire (resort sprawl). In all, about 600 miles of the 2,600 miles of coast fall into this category (see Table 6:5).[14]

Table 6:5

Types of coastline and competing users (generalised)

Type	Percentage	Agriculture	Industry	Recreation	Conservation
Cliffs over 50 ft high	33	x		x	xx
Cliffs under 50 ft high	6	x		x	
Dunes	9		x	xx	xx
Marsh	11	xx	xx		xx
Shingle	20		x	x	x
Built up	22		xx	x	

x = Land-use interest   xx = Strong land-use interest

In the past, conflicts of interest were few, thanks to the concentration of activity in a few places. What was a good site for a port for example was often a poor one for a resort. At present, the growing pressure of recreation is matched by increased demands by agriculture and by industry, especially large-scale modern industry, for coastal land. Although conflicts exist between all three categories of demand and within each, most attention has been focused on their mutual clash with the conservation interest. This is especially important in areas of great natural beauty (the term is here more appropriate than in a rural context) such as high cliff areas, or in areas of unusual ecological conditions, such as marshes and sanddunes. It is this type of coast which Rawnsley 'assume[s] enlightened opinion would wish to be preserved'.[15]

Although such industrial developments as the oil refineries of Pembrokeshire and the aluminium smelter at Holyhead have been important issues, the most insidious enemy of conservation has been recreation itself, especially in the form of the non-traditional type of holiday. The caravan, Rawnsley's 'new abomination', and the small, rather informal (to be kind) holiday cottage have been the two most consistent targets of the conservationists.[16] Although there is considerable logic on the side of those who argue that such forms of development must be rigorously restricted (since for example it is physically impossible for everyone to have his own caravan/shack at the coast), it is perhaps unfortunate that their arguments are directed at the lower-middle class type of holiday. The holiday cottage at £5,000 and the town hotel—the two major bases of the wealthy holiday-maker—are not considered undesirable. As with the countryside, the planning of the coastline has intrinsically favoured the wealthy, although it is difficult to see what other course could have been taken.

The main policies of the planners of the coast in recent years have been based on attempts 'to maximise the potentialities of the already built-up areas and . . . to [attempt] to clamp down on every development in the very small areas of open coastline [remaining]'.[17] It will be readily appreciated that this is exactly the opposite of the exhibited tendency of recreational coastal use. It is also a policy similar to that adopted in rural areas. However, unlike the latter, the given resources of the coastal areas are known to be strictly limited and to be totally insufficient for free use. If anything then the case for coastal planning is much stronger than the one, which is also reasonable, for rural recreational planning.

Yet little specific legislation has been made for coastal areas. Protection in one form or another (the National Trust, the Countryside Commission, Nature Conservancy, Forestry Commission, Duchy and Crown Lands, Ministry of Defence) covers approximately 1,300 miles of coast. However, the degrees of protection offered are extremely varied and the value, for instance, of Ministry of Defence 'protection' in Pembrokeshire has often been questioned. The task of protection is practically in the hands of the local planning authorities who are rarely in a position to co-ordinate the multiple protecting agencies.

The extent of protection is greatest in those regions where pressure on coastal land use, although considerable, is not as critical as in areas close to major urban centres. Thus the counties with most protection are Pembroke, Devon, Anglesey, Cornwall, and Cardigan, all over 80 per cent 'safeguarded'.[18] These regional variations in demand and supply would give scope for manœuvre as far as national coastal planning if the effective apparatus for such planning were available.

THE HOLIDAY RESORTS

From 1801 to 1951 the holiday resorts were the most rapidly growing urban places. Since the latter date their growth has apparently slowed. However, as usual we must qualify this statement. The average growth rate of County Boroughs in England and Wales 1951–69 has been approximately 4·8 per cent whilst that of those County Boroughs which are known primarily as holiday resorts has been 4·3 per cent. Although in some cases growth has been 'retarded' by overspill from the centre of resorts to surrounding areas, nevertheless the figures do reflect their changing status. Some of the smaller resorts still show rapid growth but this too masks a functional change in the direction of retirement towns—quiet respiration rather than rejuvenating inspiration is their *métier*.

Seasonal unemployment has long been a problem in coastal resort towns. As one example amongst the many that could be given, unemployment at Rhyl, January 1965, was over two and a half times the national figure. Now, it is true that 'seasonality of recreational demands on the . . . coast is diminishing',[19] especially in areas close to urban populations. But this spread of season exactly mirrors the spatial spread of activities—that is it has little effect on this basic problem of the large resorts.

Although the resorts have 85 per cent of holiday accommodation they cater for only 65 per cent of the holiday-makers.[20] Over 60 per cent of these still take their main holiday in July and August (see Table 6:6). The spread of seasonality applies to the casual short stay visit which, as we have seen, is directed often towards dispersed holiday areas, and during which expenditure is minimal.

Table 6:6

Holiday seasons

Taking holiday	1951 (%)	1962 (%)	1968 (%)
July–August	64	63	62
May–September	96	97	96

Source: BTA. op. cit.

The attitude of Lindsey County Council therefore in respect of Cleethorpes, Skegness, and Mablethorpe is widespread; they expressed the hope that the Greater London Council overspill schemes would create 'a broadening of the industrial and employment base of towns where less dependence on the holiday industry would seem to be desirable'.[21] Similarly, in each of the Yorkshire resorts industrial estates have been created as they have been at Eastbourne; engineering/electronics industry has clustered at Torquay; land along the railway in Hove and Portslade has been industrialised;[22] engineering, clothing and heavy industries (Prestatyn) have been established in North Wales resorts; Blackpool has important transport equipment and food industries as have Lowestoft and Great Yarmouth; the Ayrshire coastal resorts are actively encouraging industrial development; Minehead has its share of the Severnside aeronautical industry. Most of these developments are modest, viewed nationally, and have rarely transformed employment patterns. They have been important enough locally to raise doubts in conservation circles.

The continued popularity of the resorts with day trippers is far from being a blessing. Socially, conflict arises between residents, who are often retired persons, and visitors, often young city dwellers. Economically, the concentration of facilities at one point originally intended for staying visitors is the attraction. In essence this is exactly the same problem faced in National Parks, and as with the latter little has been done to solve the problem. Mention, however, has been made of grants towards facilities on the south-east coast being made by the GLC. The demands on these facilities far outweighs the payment made towards them by daytrippers. To take one example, Bexhill has eleven times as many day visitors as resident

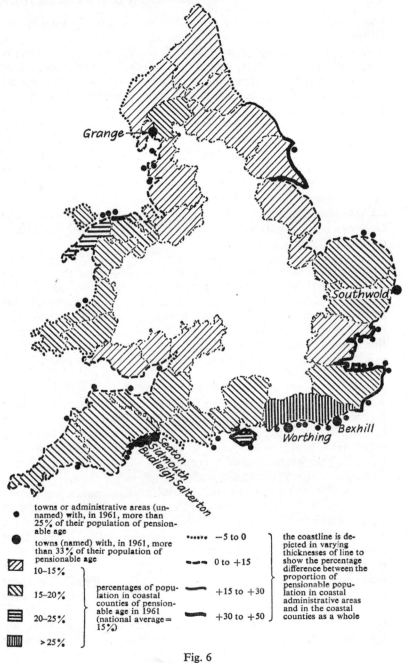

Grange

Southwold

Worthing   Bexhill

Seaton
Sidmouth
Budleigh Salterton

- towns or administrative areas (un-
  named) with, in 1961, more than
  25% of their population of pensionable age

● towns (named) with, in 1961, more
  than 33% of their population of
  pensionable age

▨ 10–15% ⎫
▧ 15–20% ⎬ percentages of popu-
▤ 20–25% ⎪ lation in coastal
▥ >25% ⎭ counties of pension-
             able age in 1961
             (national average=
             15%)

•••••• −5 to 0

- - - 0 to +15

━━━ +15 to +30

━━━ +30 to +50

the coastline is de-
picted in varying
thicknesses of line to
show the percentage
difference between the
proportion of
pensionable popu-
lation in coastal
administrative areas
and in the coastal
counties as a whole

Fig. 6

Pensioners on the Coast

holidaymakers, yet the latter provide 70 per cent of the total tourist revenue.[23]

A geography of old age in Britain would find itself primarily concerned with the coast, especially with the smaller resorts. This phenomenon of retirement to the coast is not new but has grown rapidly since 1951. In Bexhill, for example, pensionable population in that year accounted for 25·8 per cent of the population as a whole; by 1961 the figure was 37·0 per cent. Whilst pensioners totalled 14·9 per cent of the population of England and Wales in 1961, seven coastal administrative areas had figures of over 33·3 per cent and forty-seven of over 25 per cent. All the seven were small towns as opposed to large resorts or rural areas; only one of these was in the north of England whilst three were in East Devon. Few counties do not show this clustering of old people along the coast. The tendency is least marked in south and west Wales, and in much of northern England.

These elderly migrants seldom choose resorts for their retirement which are less than 60 miles from their homes[24]—often they move to places more than 200 miles away. With them they bring the need for special amenities, notably medical ones. Some resorts have felt that this form of migration has upset a healthy population structure and partly justify their attempts to attract industry as a means to rectify this situation. Since many of the retirement resorts are relatively small towns, their attractions for industry are rather restricted.

Devon and Cornwall: an illustrative example

Although the south-west peninsula of Britain does not entirely typify all these general problems, especially insofar as it is not an important day trip destination, its recent development illustrates many such problems empirically. In 1947 Pimlott expressed the belief that the masses would never come to the region.[25] Today, it is increasingly the most popular holiday region in Britain.

In 1965 it was estimated that coastal holiday-makers accounted for 85 per cent of all visitors to the region, whilst only 5 per cent were visitors to Dartmoor.[26] The South West Region of the BTA as a whole received 8·3 million holiday-makers in 1968 (including an estimated 1·7 million who were taking an additional holiday) spending approximately £105 million. Devon and Cornwall on their own received 5·5 million visitors who spent £70 million.[27] The latter sum is rather more than the total value of manufacturing industry to the region and is equivalent to £60 per head of population in the two counties. At peak periods for every ten inhabitants there are 5·8 visitors in Cornwall and 2·9 in Devon.[28] Indeed, in 1966 visitors exceeded residents in several areas: in Newquay there were 2·45 per inhabitant, in Polperro 2·20, along the Camel estuary and at Boscastle 1·60, and at St Ives 1·34. In Cornwall, of the total work force of 135,000, 11·2 per cent is directly engaged in the holiday industry.[29] To understate the case Devon and Cornwall have an increasingly important stake in coastal recreation.

This increasing pressure is not without its problems. In the railway era the region was not particularly accessible, especially so along its northern coast. At present, however, over 80 per cent of visitors arrive by car[30] and formerly neglected areas are now amongst the most popular. Whilst the car has brought new prosperity to ancient fishing villages it has also brought problems. Clovelly has avoided these by banning the car altogether, other towns have provided large parking areas to retain custom. St Ives, for example, had over one car space for every two inhabitants in 1966 which gave it traffic problems twenty years in advance of those faced in the rest of Britain.[31] The cost of the provision of each space is estimated at £100, a capital outlay in the St Ives case of £50 per person or about £125 per ratepayer. Such expenditure, on only one type of public facility provision, is not recovered through visitor spending. The profit per year of each space is about £3 in urban areas and £5 (assuming that fees can be collected) in rural areas. In either case at present interest rates, the facility is hardly self-supporting.

A second problem is that neither employment nor resident resort population has increased proportionately to the increasing number of visitors. Whilst tourist expenditure in Cornwall rose by 66 per cent during 1951–61 direct employment in the industry rose by less than 15 per cent. In itself this can be taken to mean increased gross revenue per inhabitant. It also means increased per capita expenditure on facilities. Although the increase in the number of visitors to the South West since 1945 is comparable to any nineteenth-century holiday boom, it is not reflected in similar town growth. Firstly because much of the increase in employment that has taken place has been outside the towns and, second, since 1921, direct employment expressed as a percentage of total employment has in fact fallen in Cornwall as a whole but most markedly in the urban areas.[32]

This is partly explained by the changing nature of the holiday. Whilst hotels, guest and boarding houses accounted for 64 per cent of all visitors in Cornwall in 1954, the equivalent figure in 1964 was only 47 per cent; the proportion staying in rented property and caravans rose from 13 to 29 per cent.[33] The latter types of accommodation are scattered along the whole coast.

Given such changes, discrepancies have arisen between demand

for and capacity of holiday accommodation (see Table 6:7). Total
capacity is barely adequate at peak periods, especially in Devon
where peak demand in 1966 was for over 240,000 beds with 234,000
available. In Cornwall the situation was somewhat easier with

Table 6:7

Comparison between capacity and demand in Cornwall
1966

Type	% of total capacity	% of total demand (satisfied)
Hotels	18	23
Bed and breakfast	38	31
Camping	10	9
Caravans/Chalets	24	29
Others	10	7

Sources: derived from BTA 1967 and Heck 1966.

232,000 beds for only slightly more than 200,000 visitors.[34] These
total figures conceal wide disparities between different types of
accommodation. Whilst caravan and hotel holidays continue to
remain undersupplied the small guest house is seriously short of
custom. Since most of the proprietors of the latter form a large
proportion of urban ratepayers—unlike hoteliers and their often
'imported' employees—the problem of increased demands on ratepayers for facility provision is clearly exacerbated. As with the resorts
in the Alps (see above, p. 58), so in the South West the very rapid
increase in holiday-making has brought few tangible benefits and
many inconveniences to local inhabitants.

Partly by reason of the many external factors influencing the
holiday trade, and partly because of the limited sphere of action
within which they are able to operate, local authority planners are
rarely able to take positive action towards solutions of the abovementioned problems. Most of their attention has been directed
towards the control of the spread of the mobile holiday and the
caravan, in efforts to achieve a rational use of coastal land. Devon
and Cornwall have in some ways been fortunate in that the era of
their popularity has coincided with the introduction and extension
of physical planning in Britain.

Over sixty-five miles of the coastline is owned by the National
Trust (nearly 40 per cent of the Trust's coastal land); over 300 miles
are included in Areas of Outstanding Natural Beauty (52 per cent
of the total of such coastline in England and Wales); and of the total

'protected' coastline of England and Wales Devon and Cornwall have about 370 miles (28 %).[35] Despite this, 11 per cent of the Devon coast is now considered to be saturated by development. In such areas no further expansion is to be encouraged. Over a further 73 per cent of the coast development is being actively discouraged by virtue of its scientific interest, its 'quiet character', or in the interest of day visitors in such areas. This leaves 16 per cent of the coastline for further development and almost all of this is intended to fill spaces in or between already developed zones.[36] This policy of concentration and protection is little different from the Countryside Commission's own plans either for coasts or inland rural recreation areas.

Given the greater popularity and much more obviously finite resources of the coast, given that British society does not yet seem inclined to reject the new dictum—an Englishman's second home is no less his castle then, no matter how fatalistic it may appear, this policy of strictly containing the rather nasty forces of competitive leisure at the coast seems to be virtually the best available. Modern coastal use increasingly involves both regional and local public expenditure for an increasingly national clientele with relatively smaller returns accruing. Increased cooperation between coastal land protectors and agencies is essential whilst the submission of individual interest to socially agreed aims seems inevitable.

1. British Travel Association, 1969. *The British on Holiday.*
2. BTA/University of Keele, 1969. *Pilot National Recreation Survey Report,* no. 2.
3. Abbott, L. (CPO, Dorset), 1966. *Coastal Preservation and Development.* Report to the National Parks Commission Regional Conference.
4. Conservative Political Centre, 1966. *A Better Country.*
5. Jessop, R., 1967. *Boating in North Wales.* Unpublished M.A. thesis, Manchester University.
6. BTA/University of Keele. op. cit.
7. Rees-Pryce, W. T., 1967. The Location and Growth of Holiday Caravan Camps in Wales, *TIBG*, XLII, pp. 127–52.
8. Oxenbury, T. B., and Smith C. W. (CPO, S.E. Suffolk), 1967. *The Coast of East Suffolk.*
9. Burton, T. L., and Wibberley, G. P., 1965. *Outdoor Recreation in the British Countryside.* Wye College, London.
10. Rawnsley, C., 1965. *The Preservation of the Coast.* Paper presented at the Second Conference of the 'Countryside in 1970'.
11. BTA, 1969. op cit.
12. See, for example, National Parks Commission, 1966. *The Coasts of Kent and Sussex*, HMSO.
13. Derived from figures given in reference 12.

E

14. Rawnsley. op cit.
15. ibid.
16. National Parks Commission. op. cit.
17. ibid.
18. Burton and Wibberley. op. cit.
19. National Parks Commission. op. cit.
20. Burton and Wibberley. op. cit.
21. Stirling, R. L. (CPO, Lindsey), 1967. Report prepared for the Regional Conference on coastal preservation and development.
22. Thompson, B., 1969. Brighton's Manufacturing Industry, *Geography*, LIV, pp. 181–5.
23. National Parks Commission. op. cit.
24. Mellor, H., 1962. Retirement to the Coast, *Town Planning Review*, XXXIII, pp. 40–7.
25. Pimlott, J. A. R., 1947. *The Englishman's Holiday.*
26. Burton and Wibberley. op. cit.
27. Derived from Dower, M., 1967. *The Strategy* [for the South West] *as it affects Tourism and Recreation.* Paper read to the Town and Country Planning Association conference.
28. Lewes, F. M. M., Culyer, A., Brady, G. A., 1967. *Holiday Transport in Devon and Cornwall.* University of Exeter.
29. Heck, H. W. J. (CPO, Cornwall), 1966. *The Holiday Industry.*
30. Lewes, Culyer, Brady. op. cit.
31. ibid.
32. Heck. op. cit.
33. ibid.
34. BTA, 1967. *A Study of Holiday and Tourist Facilities in the Four South-western Counties: Interim Report.*
35. Rawnsley. op. cit.
36. Turnbull, P., 1966. The Coast of Devon *Town and Country Planning*, February; Hornsby-Smith, P. M., 1970. Camping on the Coast: the Case of Newquay, Cornwall, *Town Planning Review*, XLI.

FREE TIME IN THE CITY

The priority given to the land-use implications of recreational research has resulted in a heavy concentration in contemporary literature on problems of countryside conservation and on the provision of amenities for outdoor recreation.[1] Consequently there is little written as yet on the supply of indoor amenities in urban centres.[2] This chapter is concerned with the distribution of such facilities, with particular reference to the public sector of provision.

Rapid changes in fashion and taste mean that leisure activities sought on the open market, and made available through private investment, are the most difficult to measure and analyse. Often statistics relating to participation rates are not open to researchers, and expressed demand is then difficult to assess. For this reason, among others, most published material assesses indoor amenities provided by central, regional or local government.

The following summary of a home interview survey made on Teesside in 1965 and 1966 suggests that the population there does not lead a very active recreational life.

Projects of this kind involving questionnaire or interview techniques illustrate that a population deprived of certain aspects of recreational provision has great difficulty in verbally expressing the latent demand factor or actually has little demand. In other words, supply must be accessible before demand is expressed, and it is clear that usual methods of sociological enquiry cannot satisfactorily be applied to the relationship between supply and demand in the recreational equation. Work done in America has suggested that 'where the facilities are . . . people will use them', or that supply stimulates its own demand,[4] making possible the greater satisfaction of latent or unfulfilled demand.

Table 7:1

Daily proportion of total population engaging
in leisure activities[3]

Active outdoor recreation	1·0%
Passive outdoor recreation	4·2%
Indoor active recreation	0·9%
Cultural activities	1·2%
Visiting clubs, pubs & churches	15·1%
Social visiting	13·7%
Unspecified	7·6%

Source: Unpublished Report on Recreation in Teeside. 1966.

THE RELATIONSHIP BETWEEN SUPPLY OF AND DEMAND FOR LEISURE

It is clear that more leisure time is spent knitting, watching television, or gardening, than in any other outdoor or indoor activity. The English garden and allotment is an integral and all-pervading part of the townscape. Sadly, very little information exists on the British in their gardens. Land-use studies and reports on open spaces in towns concern themselves with public provision, although studies have been made of allotments in Oxford.[5] However, the recent appearance of the Garden Centre as an increasingly important aspect of the retail market reflects a continuing and perhaps growing interest in gardening as a recreational activity. Yet public provision plays its most important role in the supply of capital-intensive facilities in towns. If more people attend football matches than opera performances in Glasgow, it may be because there is better provision in one than the other. If such recreational patterns reflect anything at all, it is the inadequate supply of facilities and the lack of well-established leisure-time habits which have a long historical explanation where demand expressed may reflect the uneven distribution of provision.

In a recent report[6] a committee on opera and ballet concluded that 'to a large extent supply creates demand, particularly if the supply is regular and of a high quality. Potential demand also depends on the steps which are taken to encourage interest in schools and colleges, on television and radio. There has been since 1945 a most encouraging increase in all of these activities, with a satisfactory response from the general public.' This is the view from the metropolis, and it is certainly not universally held by regional and local communities who still find themselves deprived of such regular and high quality entertainment. If problems associated with unoccupied leisure could be seen in the same light as the consequences of unemployment, then the supply and redistribution of all recreational amenities would surely be treated more seriously by both central and local government authorities and given a higher place in the list of priorities for public expenditure in Britain.

Since World War II, during which most of the usual recreational amenities were not available for leisure purposes, recognition has been given to the need for *a priori* assumptions in planning the use of space for leisure in urban areas. The Local Government Act of 1948, in Section 132, enabled local authorities, except County Councils and Parish Councils, to spend up to the product of a 6d rate on the arts and entertainment. In effect this meant that municipalities were given the authority to spend up to £16 million. If one accepts the premise that the provision of the widest possible range of recreational amenities for the whole population is part of education and welfare expenditure, then there is clearly a need for a redistribution of resources. The pub, club, pop group and bowling alley are commercially successful; theatres, community and sports centres are not. In a recent study Bowen and Baumol[7] pointed out that the costs of art promotions are rising at a rate which will never be matched by income derived from performances. A symphony concert requires a large hall, a large number of skilled musicians, and their instruments, and other expensive items. This means that production costs will never fall to a level where the public could afford to pay the real price for a seat. Tickets have always been subsidised, previously by private, and more recently by public, patronage.

For these reasons, only a leisured élite could enjoy the comparative luxury of sport and the arts until the end of the last century. Even in 1914 it was still the Victorian pub, gin-palace, church or music-hall which provided entertainment in town centres for the masses.

As a matter of economic theory it might be argued that the livelihood of artists ought to be provided by the people who enjoy their work. In practice it has never been: and the actions of successive governments in this country in setting up the Arts Council and empowering local authorities to subsidise from the rates, recognise the absolute necessity, in modern times, of public patronage.[8]

Sport

If there is an obvious need to subsidise provision of the arts, then equally there is one in planning for and investing in sports facilities. The Army, Air Force and Navy were the pioneers of sports halls in Britain, and even now many halls are not generally available for public use, being still linked to the services, industry or educational establishments. This shortage is dealt with very thoroughly in two reports published at least ten years ago—the Albemarle Report on 'The Youth Service of England and Wales' and the Wolfenden Committee's 'Sport and the Community', but was first brought to the public's notice in 1956 in a report[9] which said:

1. That the level of participation in a wide range of sports had at least kept pace with the growth of population and the interest was wider.
2. That whilst outdoor facilities were perhaps just adequate, indoor facilities certainly were not.
3. That there was evidence that increased supply generates increased demand both in facilities and instruction.

The Arts

Not only was there agreement on the need to increase the level of supply of these amenities and to subsidise them with public funds, but also, of more interest to the geographer, there was recognition of the need to redistribute them. In 1960 the Arts Council described 'the deplorable dearth, outside the metropolis, of concert halls and playhouses'[10] a year after it had published a survey of existing facilities in London and the provinces. In this report[11] a model for provision outside of London recommended that every town with a population of 200,000 or over should have an art gallery, a hall(s) where concerts can adequately be given, one or two theatres, one for companies touring good quality opera, ballet and drama, and one as the home of a resident repertory.

In the sense that it took no account of regional differentials in income or socio-economic structure, this model was unworkable, but it did recommend that central funds should be redistributed in favour of the regions. As if to symbolise the need for decentralisation, the North Eastern Association for the Arts was formed in 1961. Until that date the structure of promotion of and expenditure on recreation in towns was a simple two-tier hierarchy: the Arts Council and other central bodies, and the local authorities. Although this was a period of expansion in provision for leisure in towns, the policy makers emphasised the raising of standards of provision, rather than a widespread diffusion of activity which it was thought might be 'liable to produce the dry-rot of mediocrity'. The central bodies saw radio and television as the natural agents of diffusion.

As a reaction against this centralisation of control, the regions, and particularly those at a greater distance from London, began to organise associations which could coordinate the activities of in-dividual local authorities and societies.

The South West was the first to establish a regional Arts Associ-ation, but it was not until 1961 with the appearance of the North Eastern Association of the Arts (NEAA) that an entirely new principle evolved. The Association was a federation, coordinating the activities of several local authorities, two universities, television and radio, amateur societies, adult education, etc., and was welcomed at all levels as 'a prototype of patronage'.[12]

The major aims of the new North Eastern Arts Association were:

(1) to make better known the range of artistic activities already available in the region;
(2) to encourage higher standards of production and the widest range of enjoyment;
(3) to stimulate local activity and to introduce the best artists from outside [the region].

In their first annual report NEAA stressed the importance of the development of regional arts and sports associations, saying that 'we believe we will have an increasing influence upon the standard of living in the region. The speed with which we can dispel old illusions about the North East will depend on the support we can gain from local authorities, industry, etc.'[13]

A slow process of decentralisation throughout the 1960s made more accessible a wide range of activities which had previously been concentrated in and around London, although in 1968 an Estimates Committee in the House of Commons published a substantial report on Grants for the Arts, which emphasised the continuing imbalance between the metropolis and the regions, and the growing need for a redistribution of income from grants for buildings etc. One of the main problems is the existence of legends in the minds of central administrators, journalists and others who feel that 'it would be foolish to imagine that there is in England, Wales, Scotland or Northern Ireland a ravenous public for the arts. A large section of the population is completely indifferent to anything that comes under the heading of "culture" and they have every right to stay in his state of non-grace.'[14]

If there is indifference in the regions, which is doubtful, then it must reflect the population's long and unfortunate deprivation of facilities for the kind of activity which is within reach of all those living within thirty miles of London. How can anyone be enthusiastic about opera if the nearest permanent company of international standard is three hundred miles away?

In the last ten years regional arts associations have been formed in Lincolnshire (1964), the North West (1966), North Wales (1967), Merseyside and the South in 1968, Yorkshire and the East Midlands in 1969 and in East Anglia, the West Midlands and West Wales in 1971. It is interesting to see the distribution of these regional bodies and to notice that the influence of the metropolis has extended over the Home Counties and towards Oxford up the Thames valley, so that there is still no strong local need expressed in the form of regional associations for these areas. Significantly, it was in those regions at a greater distance from the metropolitan amenities that the most progressive developments in the provision for leisure were made. This pattern is also recognisable in other fields of regional development, and it has been argued that a strong regional identity appears only when the metropolitan influences wane.

Public patronage for the arts has begun to show a more sophisticated, even molecular, structure during the 1960s, and the existence of the regional association has added a third dimension to the structure of promotion. The Arts Council sees them as 'partners in patronage' with both local and central authorities, industry, foundations like Gulbenkian, etc., the universities and radio and television. Although there are many examples of this type of corporate responsibility on the continent and in America, they have been rare in Great Britain until the last decade. This has been effected by the change in policy which now prefers the diffusion, decentralisation and dispersion of activities and amenities as its chief priority (Lord Goodman's introduction to the last Arts Council Annual Report). In a new Charter granted in 1967, the Council's aims are redefined as (1) to develop and improve the knowledge, understanding and practice of the arts; and (2) to increase the accessibility of the arts to the public throughout Great Britain.

The need for further stimulus to local government expenditure was recognised with the formation of The Sports Council and consequently of Regional Sports Councils in 1966, where representatives of local authorities and of sport will meet to discuss problems of large-scale, high-cost provision. So far they have experienced difficulty in gaining enough executive power to be effective in initiating developments. But they have already persuaded individual

Table 7:2

Socio-economic group	1	2	3	4	5	6	7	8	9	10	11	12	13	14	15	16	17
Proportion per 1,000 (1961)	36	59	8	30	39	126	9	33	316	147	83	34	10	10	23	20	17
Proportion per 1,000 (1966)	38	60	7	38	45	126	10	36	315	149	83	34	8	9	21	15	5

Sources: 1961 and 1966 Census Reports. GRO.

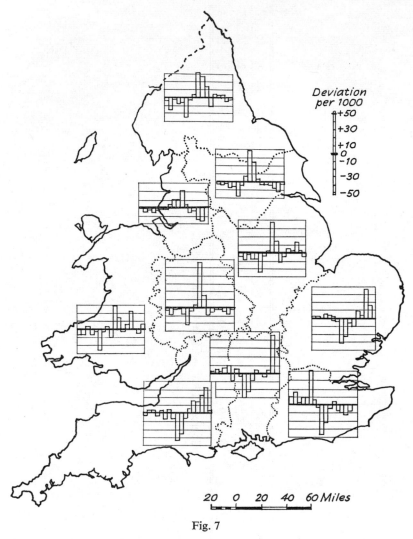

Fig. 7

Regional variations in the socio-economic structure of England and
Wales in 1961

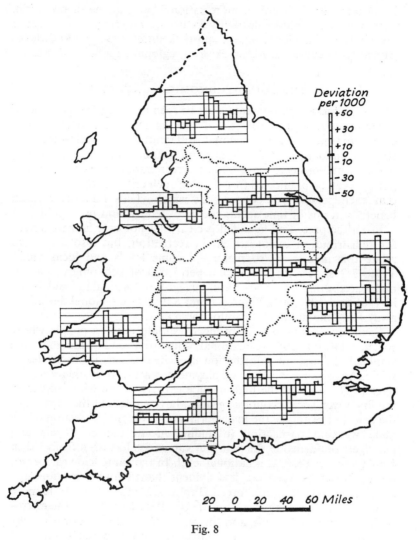

Deviation
per 1000
+50
+30
+10
0
-10
-30
-50

20   0   20   40   60 Miles

Fig. 8

Regional variations in the socio-economic structure of England and
Wales in 1966

local authorities towards a more rational programme of provision, with a greater built-in flexibility in use of buildings, and a better distribution of a wider range of sports facilities, based on knowledge gained from surveys done on existing regional supplies and needs.

THE SOCIO-ECONOMIC CONTEXT

However, these developments must be seen against a background of other criteria. In any analysis of the demand for and the supply of leisure-time facilities, regional differentials in socio-economic structure and income are important. Implicit in the assumption, made by numerous researchers in the recreational field, that activity patterns can be predicated from a set of such criteria is the hypothesis that each person will choose that which yields him the greatest benefit in terms of time spent, energy expended and price paid.

From the preceding figures it is clear that not only is there a need for redistribution of investment in recreation, but also a need to relate this investment to regional income levels and local needs. Table 7:2 shows the proportion per 1,000 of economically active males according to the socio-economic group, for England and Wales in 1961 and 1966, and Figures 7 and 8 illustrate regional deviations away from the national mean for these dates.

Each socio-economic group ideally should contain people whose social, cultural and recreational standards and behaviour are similar.[15] In fact the information used in this classification clearly relates to occupation and employment status. It is therefore interesting to see that the high income earners, those who fall within the first seven socio-economic groups, have gained, at the expense of the rest. For example, the managerial and professional section of the male working population (excluding group 13: employers and managers on farms) in the first four categories has risen from 133 in 1961 to 143 in 1966, at a national level. In the same five-year period the contrasts between the less affluent North and West and the South East have been reinforced. Tables 7:3 and 7:4 illustrate more precisely the dichotomous nature of the difference between the metropolitan-dominated South, and the rest of the country. For example, the Northern Region has a negative deviation in the managerial and professional sector of −33 in 1966 and of −37 in 1966, whereas London and the South East has a positive deviation of +35 in both census counts.

The same contrasts appear in an examination of the spatial distribution of personal incomes for each standard region which accentuate the nature of the dichotomy already illustrated by the

Table 7:3

Regional deviations from National Mean
(Census 1961)

Region	1–4 Managerial and Professional A	5–7 Non-Manual B	8–11 Manual C
London & South East	+35	+59	−68
Southern	+11	+3	−68
Eastern	+6	+2	−66
South Western	−8	−4	−80
North Western	−8	−4	+51
East & West Ridings	−18	−29	+78
Midlands	−20	−34	+37
North Midlands	−22	−34	+45
Wales	−25	−35	+33
Northern	−33	−37	+80

Table 7:4

Regional deviations from National Mean
(Census 1966)

Region	1–4 Managerial and Professional A	5–7 Non-Manual B	8–11 Manual C
London & South East	+35	+43	−72
South West	−9	−7	−61
East Anglia	−27	−33	−72
North West	−11	−4	+44
West Midlands	−16	−33	+57
Yorkshire & Humberside	−22	−31	+70
East Midlands	−25	−32	+48
Wales	−31	−35	+37
Northern	−37	−29	+72

Table 7:5

Region	Under £500	£500 –£999	£1,000 –£1,499	£1,500 –£1,999	£2,000 –£4,999	Over £5,000
London & South East	−6·9	−4·9	+25·5	+38·8	+44·8	+70
North	−1·1	+8·9	−23·7	−36·6	−27·7	−35

Source: Inland Revenue Statistics, 1959.

socio-economic statistics. A report from the Inland Revenue in 1967 shows that, despite a slowing down in the concentration in the South of higher income earners during the early 1960s,[16] the income differential between the South East and the North has been sustained.

Table 7:6

Region	Index of average net income before tax 1959–60	Index of average net income before tax 1964–5	Regional surpluses and deficits before tax 1964–5 (£m.) Total net income	Regional surpluses and deficits before tax 1964–5 (£m.) Net investment income
UK	100	100	0	0
South East	111	110	+482	+141
North	94	93	−79	−26

Source: Inland Revenue Statistics, 1964.

These figures do provide evidence that 'there are large and harmful differences over the United Kingdom that should be measured properly, so that well-informed action may be taken to enable the country to use or dispose of its resources to better economic and social effect'.[17]

THE HIERARCHY OF RECREATIONAL PROVISION

In a situation like that of Great Britain where there is an acknowledged spatial imbalance in the provision of recreational facilities and a dearth of published analyses of the needs of the urban population for recreation within cities, there is an obvious need for theoretical frameworks of analysis. Since the provision of recreational services in towns constitutes a no less important aspect of urban provision for its population than shopping, banking and government facilities, these too are susceptible, like those facilities, to geographical analysis. Certainly recreation provides unique problems like its non-profit-making nature (ballet, opera, etc.), but there is a case for applying the tools of geographical analysis to urban recreational needs.

It has been shown that London is a clear example of metropolitan dominance in the arts and recreation generally. In all respects, from international sporting events to first releases of new films, London has an established primacy as it has in all aspects of the British urban system. Below the metropolis there exists a hierarchy of cities ranked according to size, economic function and dominance over their hinterlands. In establishing the arrangement of such systems of cities geographers have made use of a Central Place Theory. Such a theory is developed from a consideration of the 'range' of a given good, in terms of its demand at a given price at a specific location. For any one good a network of central places of equal accessibility is produced, and by considering differently priced goods with different demand curves a hierarchy of central places evolves. Put most simply, this theory is the product of a series of spatial demand curves.

The value of a theoretical hierarchy of urban places is that it may be tested against reality and the ideal system matched against the existing system to highlight gaps in the present network of provision. The first part of this section will show the difference between an ideal distribution of central places for one good (in this case opera) and the existing system and show how, with a better set of statistics, such a study could be undertaken for all recreational goods, at a national level.

A second value of the theory is that it provides us with a general urban system based on a large number of variables. In 1944 Smailes produced a picture of the British urban hierarchy based on indices which included cinemas, banks, etc., and his work has recently been brought up to date, without major changes, by R. D. P. Smith.[18] Out of thirty-five measures of centrality (see Smith, Table 1, p. 3) the fact that only four refer to urban leisure needs is some indication of a general underprovision of subsidised facilities in the national urban network. Again this could be analysed at a national level, but will be briefly discussed here for the Southern region only.

Finally at a local level, in this case urban Teesside, it is possible to see how a theory of intra-urban central places may be developed to assess the lowest level of the national, regional and local pyramid. The analysis of Teesside highlights the problem in using the ideas developed in Central Place Theory in urban recreational analysis: the concept of the range of a good. If, as noted above, the range of a good is the product of a spatial demand curve then we are up against the immediate problem of our inability to assess demand in a situation of non-provision. There is inadequate information at this time for constructing the range of given recreational 'goods' but some of the results of a study of the arts and recreation in Urban Teesside, a place better provided for than many urban centres in England, gives us some idea of what these ranges might be. As a result of inadequacies of statistics and defined ranges the examples below are crude and intended only as an indication of the possibilities for geographical application to research into recreational needs in towns.

The national network

At a national level we may take opera as the highest value good.[19] To a degree the reason for its being so is existing demand which may not be the same as latent demand and therefore invalid as a definition of range. However, research[20] has noted that activities have an attraction at a given period of time available for participation according to a relationship between time taken in the actual activity and time taken to travel to that facility. The ratios between maximum total travel times and activity time may be summarised as in Table 7:7.

Table 7:7

Facility	Travel	:	Activity
Local	1	:	3
Sub-regional	1	:	1·5
Regional	1	:	1
National	1	:	0·7

Source: Unpublished Teesside Home Interview Survey.

Obviously the definition of national, regional and local beg the question of supply and demand. However, it is fairly obvious that opera is inherently less accessible in terms of cost of production and appreciation than much that falls under the umbrella of 'pop' culture.

If we accept opera as a national activity, then according to the above figures people would be prepared to travel a total of four hours and twenty minutes for a three-hour opera. Thus the range of opera may be defined as a time/distance function of four hours and twenty minutes. Alternatively, *The Arts in the South* report suggested a ratio of one permanent, professional opera company for a population of ten million. Because of the lack of empirical studies and the difficulties involved in measuring demand levels, such arbitrary figures must suffice as the basis for further investigation.

Using the time/distance and the population ratios, six opera companies would be a minimum national provision. Of the five in existence now, two are located in London, at Covent Garden and the Coliseum, and another is in Sussex but depends on the same metropolitan market. The Welsh National Opera has its headquarters in Cardiff and Scottish Opera in Glasgow, although neither has its own opera house.

Theoretically, the six companies which would provide the required national framework should have permanent accommodation at the point of highest accessibility to their catchment area of ten million who live within a return journey which may last up to four hours and twenty minutes. Taking Smith's revised statement of Smailes' urban system as the existing hierarchy,[21] then the opera houses should be sited in London, Birmingham, Glasgow, Manchester, Liverpool and Newcastle-on-Tyne. If national boundaries and existing lines of access from more remote areas of demand are included as locational factors, then this pattern of supply needs modification.

Wales and the South West are unprovided for in this urban hierarchy, while the population in South Lancashire would have two companies within thirty miles of each other. Thus it would seem logical to build in Cardiff rather than Liverpool. Recent migration figures also indicate faster growth rates in the South West.[22] It is appropriate to mention here that the British system is not a closed one, in so far as opera artists exist in an international labour market, and thus London is in a strong position because of its position within the first rank of world cities. This perhaps justifies the retention of two companies in the metropolis, rather than the removal of one to Birmingham.

From this brief general statement, the major gap in the present provision of this particular facility with relation to the existing urban system is in the North of England's lack of a permanent opera company. In a recent Arts Council report,[23] it was recommended that a company be created to perform in the North and that three new opera houses be built in Glasgow, Cardiff and Manchester, in order that 'operatic entities on a regional basis' could be established.

A further application of central place theory can be made with reference to the four major companies which tour throughout

Great Britain from their bases in London, Sussex, South Wales
and Scotland. The following table illustrates the location of all opera
performances given by them during two seasons.

Table 7:8

No. of performances given during the 1967–8 and 1968–9 seasons

	London*	Provinces	Abroad
Sadler's Wells	472	294	7
Glyndebourne	121	54	16
Welsh National	—	148	—
Scottish	—	95	2

Source: Arts Council Opera and Ballet Report, 1969.[24]

* Including Sussex, where the Glyndebourne Opera House is located.

There are, of course, many small companies either touring in or
indigenous to the provinces which provide operatic performances,
but for the purposes of this analysis it is those of an international
standard which are defined as the primate good. Within the obvious
limitations imposed by inadequate accommodation on tour, they
offer such standards to regional populations which would otherwise
be outside the metropolitan catchment area. The policy of the
Glyndebourne touring opera is defined as giving 'regional audiences
an opportunity to hear operas which they may or may not have
heard in translation, in the language for which the music was
written'.[25] Traditionally, Sadler's Wells has performed operas in
English and in this way offers a complementary service to provincial
populations. The Welsh and Scottish touring companies try to cover
areas visited infrequently by the other tours, and as yet have concentrated their activities in the North and West. Neither limits itself
to its own 'national' territory, however, and is therefore providing an
invaluable part of British provision. More recently there has been a
move towards rationalisation of tours because companies find that
provincial facilities are inadequate and that their standards fall as a
result: the nature of the service is therefore changing.

The regional network

To carry the study of urban provision for leisure to a regional level
rather than a national one, we may see the skeleton of a hierarchy
reproduced. Again, lack of statistics and their variable nature
prevent a real analysis at this point, but indicators of the type of
analysis possible may be discovered.

There are two recreational councils operating in what may be described as Southern England, that is, the area between the metropolitan region and the West Country, an ill-defined part of England in terms of physical, urban or cultural unity unlike its neighbours to the East and West. The Southern Arts Association and the Southern Sports Council both work in the area but their boundaries are rather different. The former includes Hampshire, Berkshire, West Sussex and Wiltshire, while the latter caters for Oxfordshire and Buckinghamshire but has no responsibility for West Sussex or Wiltshire. This makes a comparison of their published figures available only for Hampshire and Berkshire. Both councils have published reports within a year of each other,[26] with some analysis of the provision of subsidised indoor leisure facilities. The following analysis rests on the basis of these two reports.

The five facilities which will be used for a comparison of provision in the central places of these countries are theatres, art galleries, musical societies affiliated to the National Federation of Music Societies, indoor sports centres and indoor swimming pools. Theatres are taken as all types, even those open only in summer as well as those planned or to be converted[27] and, while music societies may not have permanent premises for performance, they do provide a facility for the musical public. The definitions are crude but provide a first indication of the provision in these two counties. A further qualification must be made. This is that the catchment areas mapped by the Southern Sports Council in its 1970 report have been applied to facilities for the arts, to group all under one town; thus the art gallery at Christchurch is placed with Bournemouth.

When these facilities are grouped together a hierarchy of provision in central places throughout Hampshire and Berkshire emerges, with a definite break between the four largest towns and the rest, and another more arbitrary break between towns with two facilities and those with only one where this may be simply the result of chance factors. An example of this latter group would be the establishment of a private gallery by an individual benefactor.

The four first-order centres defined by subsidised leisure provision are Bournemouth, Reading, Southampton and Portsmouth, in that order. These are the dominant centres of population in the region and are defined by Smith as cities, with Southampton as a major city. In this context Southampton seems under-provided although Bournemouth's history as a South Coast resort with a permanent symphony orchestra gives it a tradition of leisure activity. Reading's position is artifically strengthened by its large number of music societies. If any inference may be made from this regional picture it is that lower second and higher third order centres in the national British urban hierarchy have between ten and fifteen publicly subsidised recreational facilities. As a general number this seems low for cities with a population of over 100,000 serving a regional population.

The Southern region has a gap in the general urban hierarchy corresponding to Smith's 3b rank, and this is reflected in the gap between the four largest centres and the second group with between three and six facilities. The second group in Table 7:9 are all major towns of the lowest order (3c) or towns of the highest order (4a) except for Abingdon and Wantage, both of which seem over-provided in relation to the general regional situation. Since Abingdon is within fifteen minutes' drive of Oxford, one of the best provided leisure centres in the country, its position seems particularly anomalous.

The lowest group of centres correspond in general to Smith's smaller towns (4b and 4c) with one major exception. Aldershot is in the third order of Smith's urban system which corresponds to Smailes' minor cities and major towns yet has only one facility in the public sector of provision. It is thus ranked with sub-towns like Ringwood and Lymington. Bracknell, a new town noted by Smith as an example of how a new town may develop central place functions, seems underprovided for as yet. Romsey and Hungerford are the only sizeable centres in the region with none of these facilities. Both are on the western boundary of the region with no large centre except Salisbury to provide for their populations.

A concentration of facilities suggests the existence of a 'cultural belt' along the Thames around Maidenhead and Windsor, and a pronounced lack of facilities in the west of the area, relative to the east. The ubiquitous nature of music societies indicates that this has the lowest range of all the recreational 'goods' under consideration. People set them up locally rather than move to join one in a larger place. Obviously this is the only facility that requires no public investment and may be indulged in easily by private individuals collecting in a house. If this element is taken out of the criteria, a large number of the places in the lower range of the hierarchy disappears and the dominance of the upper parts increases. There is a serious under-provision, especially in sports facilities indoors, in the region. This is admitted by the Southern Sports Council in its report. The lack of indoor sports centres, so well provided for in urban Teesside, is especially acute in the highly urbanised South Coastal part of Hampshire. Admittedly the weather and sea provide far more outdoor activity than is possible for the North East but that none of the three major urban centres has an indoor sports centre is an indication of inadequacy of central place recreational function of places at the top of the regional urban hierarchy.

The Southern region is of course within easy reach of the metropolis. This both explains and in part justifies the lack of provision

Table 7:9

Place	No. of facilities	Place in Smith's hierarchy
Bournemouth	14	3a
Reading	13	3a
Southampton	11	2c
Portsmouth	10	3a
Basingstoke	6	3c
Winchester	5	3c
Abingdon	5	4b
Windsor	4	3c
Maidenhead	4	4a
Newbury	3	3c
Petersfield	3	4a
Wantage	3	4c
Alton	2	4b
Andover	2	4a
Aldershot	1	3c
Bracknell	1	4a
Wallingford	1	4c
Wokingham	1	4b
Lymington	1	4b
Ringwood	1	4c

Categories according to Smith's hierarchy:

2c—city
3a—major towns (large)
3c—major towns (small)
4(a,b)—towns
4c—sub-towns

Sources:

1. Duncan, N. S., 1969. *The Arts in the South.*
2. Southern Sports Council, May 1970.
3. Smith, R. D. P., 1968. The changing urban hierarchy, *Regional Studies*, vol. 2., pp. 1–19.

for indoor recreation. With two motorways to London to be completed by the end of the 1970s through the region (M3 and M4) this access will increase. However, the nature of such activities as swimming, basketball, squash and local theatre is that it should be easily accessible to the greatest number of people and this is possible only within the regional centres. To have a large gap in such provision in towns like Southampton, Portsmouth and Reading, to say nothing of the lesser centres like Newbury and Aldershot, is to make nonsense of a hierarchy of provision based upon range of goods as well as to make such places lesser centres in a regionally balanced economy.

Little has been said here of the 'range' of recreational goods. This is perhaps the most difficult to assess (certainly it is impossible in the present situation of ignorance of demand and supply factors), and yet the most useful tool for analysis of provision. An adequate application of central place theory has the potential to place the study of urban recreation in the United Kingdom on a far surer footing, but must await more detailed knowledge of the range of recreational goods. Studies of Teesside and of the intra-urban provision of indoor leisure facilities give some indication of such ranges in a place where these facilities have been better provided than in most non-metropolitan urban centres in England and it is to this level of the national hierarchy that we now turn.

TEESSIDE: AN INTRA-URBAN RECREATIONAL SYSTEM

If the demand for and supply of leisure facilities in towns may be studied at a national or inter-urban level then it is also possible to analyse them in greater detail inside one of the major urban centres. Similarly the more local 'good' and its range may be studied to provide an inter-urban central place network. The provision of swimming pools, sports stadia and theatres within the urban area provides the basis for such a study.

The new Teesside County Borough with a population approaching 400,000 is made up of a number of traditionally independent centres and thus faces an historical problem of competition between these centres in provision and the resulting lack of centralised amenities best sited for the benefit of the population of the conurbation as a whole. The city still lies outside the national touring circuit for opera, ballet and large-scale dramatic productions, it is below the national mean in terms of a number of socio-economic variables, but has recently developed a strong tradition of local provision for urban recreation.

A history of recreational provision

It is possible to see a number of phases in the changing provision of facilities for recreation in urban Teesside since the beginning of this century. Traditionally the pub, the club, and the church have provided a focus for community life in a population which was mainly working class. Whereas public libraries, museums and swimming baths were built during the last fifty years of the nineteenth century with local authority funds, few other recreational facilities were provided during a period when for most people leisure time was spent making excursions on Sundays and Bank Holidays to Redcar and other resorts on the North Yorkshire coast.

Before 1914, it was only those living in the wealthier Teesside suburbs who could afford the luxury of private golf, tennis or other sports clubs, which was all that the towns offered as an alternative to the scarce public facilities or the decadence of gin palaces. In *Recreations* J. A. R. Pimlott suggests that

the cult of sport did not originate in the pedagogical theories of Dr Arnold, and other progressive headmasters, nor in a conscious or unconscious attempt to train men for the responsibilities of an emergent Empire. It seems to have arisen from the spontaneous reactions of many people to the needs of an industrial and urbanised society with a puritanical and competitive ethic. Sport provided channels for the energies of youth, whether confined within boarding school or city streets, which were less degrading and less damaging to society than hooliganism, gambling, drink and indiscriminate sex.

Although Pimlott's theory has some validity, until 1900, with the exception of Association Football, most sports were identified with the upper, and upper middle classes.

The years between the end of World War I and the mid-'fifties may be described as 'the age of the spectator'.[28] Theatres were converted to cinemas, new cinemas were built, attendances at football and cricket matches rose rapidly, greyhound and speedway stadia gained in popularity. Finally television emerged as the major recreational 'activity' of the post-war era. It is perhaps relevant to say at this point that 'active' recreation has so far remained an ill-defined concept. The authors of the Pilot National Recreation Survey state that driving a car, and social and cultural activities are not included in the category of recreation which they call 'active', and they also point out that only one person in ten engaged in any significant form of active 'from-home' recreation at week-ends. There is little doubt that radio, television, the boom in record sales and other 'at-home' distractions have contributed to a very large extent to the rise of the 'age of the spectator', although there is some evidence which suggests that towards the end of the 'fifties there was a renewal of interest in 'active' leisure-time pursuits. Numbers of those participating in a wide variety of sports grew rapidly until the legacy of Victorian and interwar facilities became inadequate. It is not difficult to explain why local authorities spent so little on sport immediately after World War II. Housing and large-scale urban renewal programmes were understandably receiving priority treatment during the late 'forties and 'fifties. However, as soon as funds became available for expenditure on recreational amenities the Teesside authorities led a national movement towards better public provision for sport.

Developments in the last decade

The last stage, since 1963, has been one of large-scale building and as such will be the period to receive most attention here. Until this date Teesside had been severely deficient in facilities for the leisure needs of its urban population. In 1970, however, no other conurbation with less than half a million people had three multi-sports centres and will have five by 1975. These are scattered throughout the urban region serving an intra-urban network with central places. Between 1860 and 1960, less was achieved than has been achieved during the last seven years, and from a position well below the national mean Teesside has risen to the exalted ranks of one of the leaders in local authority sports provision in Great Britain.

Each week an average of 30,000 people pass through the doors of the sports centres on Teesside. Most of those attending will participate in the activities; some will seek no more than the vicarious pleasure of watching other people enjoying themselves, and will be content to be part of a pleasantly gregarious atmosphere. The Wolfenden Report described the multi-sports centre as a 'centre of community social life: there should be advantages in family membership. The young person uncommitteed to any particular sport might by one single act of joining be enabled to try his hand at several. Such centres could certainly bring separate sports and their participants closer together.'

There is little doubt that the sports centre is already competing with the church, the pub, and the working men's club as a focus of community activity. However, it is not yet clear whether the juxtaposition of a variety of sports facilities provokes a higher degree of participation in all or any one of them, simply because the swimmer will feel moved to play squash during the same visit to the centre. Although the cohabitation of a variety of activities in the same

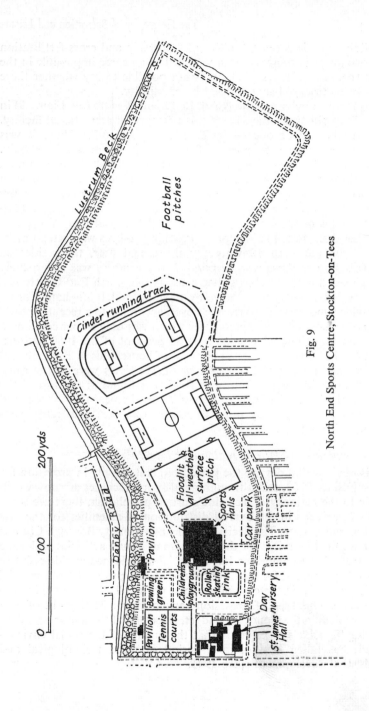

Fig. 9

North End Sports Centre, Stockton-on-Tees

building provides opportunities of fellowship and cross-fertilisation of groups of participants in a way and to a degree impossible in the old separatist arrangements, it is not possible to say whether these opportunities are being realised by a majority.

A further analysis of the North End Sports Centre (see Figure 9) in Stockton illustrates the role of this new type of recreational facility. As the first to be opened in Teesside in September 1966, it was originally intended to provide for the residents in Stockton only. As Figure 10 shows, however, it acts as a central place for the urban core of Teesside. The centre itself discovered, in a survey made in February 1967, that of those attending during one week, as many came from between four and six miles away as from within a two-mile radius of the centre. It is obvious that casual users will travel further than those in clubs or on coaching courses who attend more regularly, but even allowing for the casual user, the residential distribution of those who responded to the survey was surprisingly dispersed. Figure 11 shows that whereas the North End Centre is a city-region facility, the Thornaby Pavilion and Billingham Forum provide a more local service. However, according to a recent report[29] Teesside had an income per earner which was only 94 per cent and a per capita income which was only 85 per cent of the 1966 national figures. For the same date 54 per cent of households in England and Wales had no car and 65 per cent of Teesside's were in the same position. Whereas the Southern Region is found at the top of the national league of affluence, Teesside must be near the bottom, and all recreational activity must be seen within these different socio-economic contexts.

Contemporary needs: city regional or local?

It is obvious that despite the period of great activity in provision for leisure since 1963, and although good sports facilities are now available to the majority of Teesside's urban population, there are some very large gaps in the overall distribution of amenities for the arts in the central core. The decision of the new County Borough Council to coordinate services for the provision of leisure activities under the control of one committee has a special significance at this point in time. The demand for facilities cannot be met entirely by commercial enterprise, and in the case of the arts, not at all, since no profit is to be made. This type of provision can no longer be thought of as a luxury item in the Council's budget, since one of the major problems facing Teesside's planners is that the quality of the social environment has fallen behind, in a period of rapid technological and industrial development since 1945.

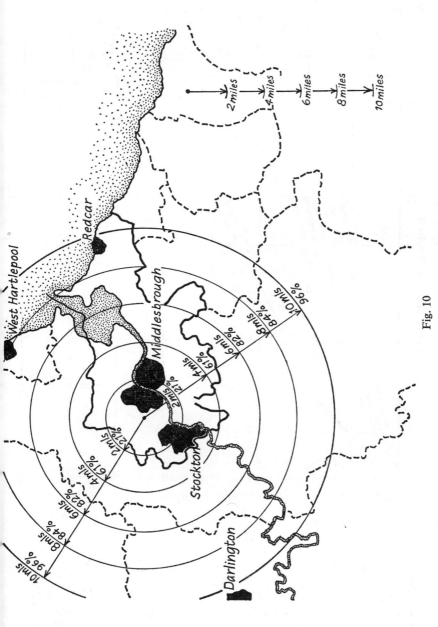

Fig. 10

Catchment area of those attending North End Sports Centre, Stockton-on-Tees

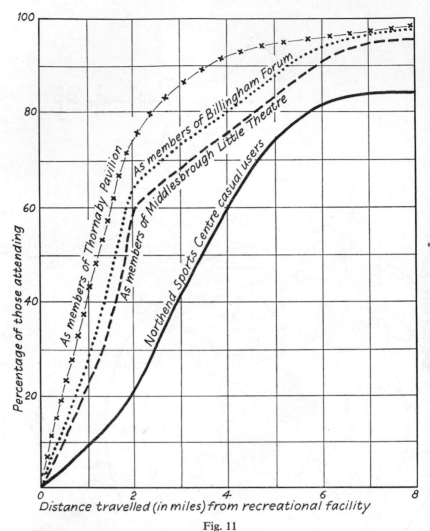

Fig. 11

Recreational mobility on Teesside, 1970

In their report to the Council, July 1969, the Department of Arts and Recreation 'recommend that the first period of five years (1970–5) should be devoted to up-grading existing facilities which are at present sub-standard . . . and to creating a balance between all services, concentrating upon provision for entertainment and all art forms'.[30] It would seem that there are two alternatives open to the Country Borough Council. They can either broaden and strengthen the base of the existing structure which evolved under the separate local authorities existing before April 1968, or they can, as part of a programme for unifying the developments of a single authority, concentrate activity in the new central area of Middlesbrough by investing in more regional facilities.

To effect the first would mean greater provision at community level, by building more amenities like the Thornaby Pavilion which, after the Thornaby Sports Centre is opened, will essentially be an arts centre for the new town residents. The proposals for extending the Middlesbrough Little Theatre facilities, by building additional workshop, rehearsal and clubrooms, is also a move in this direction. To effect the second proposal would essentially mean large-scale investment in theatre and concert-hall building in central Middlesbrough. Proposals have already been made regarding the future Civic Centre plans which include a theatre with a maximum capacity of 1,200, a concert hall of the same size, an art gallery and exhibition area to replace the existing Municipal Art Gallery in Linthorpe Road, the site of which will be required for education purposes in the near future. In addition, it would be desirable to include within this leisure complex a new Central Library to replace the existing building which has very limited space available for further extension.

If the facilities which serve the existing city region are to be extended, two developments will need to precede the building of new theatres and concert halls. First, the centre of the conurbation must be made more amenable and accessible to the population of the city region; shops must be re-located in traffic-free zones to avoid the kind of pedestrian congestion which exists now; transport facilities should be integrated into a unified system serving the new county borough as a whole, rather than the individual and separate towns which previously ran their own public transport facilities; parking areas must be extended and other services, like restaurants, improved to cope with the ancillary needs of a theatre-going public. And second, the population must begin to think of Teesside as a unit; they must develop a consciousness of their new city region.

Derek Senior[31] suggested that the problem of what is 'local' is vital in any consideration of the needs and supplies of an emergent local authority. Teesside has been called an embryonic city region[32] and it is certainly experiencing rapid change in respect of its political and administrative structure. But in the sense that any regional unit should be representative of an organic social and economic entity, the Teesside City Region is not difficult to define. Its members do have an objective community of interest, which is first and more immediately recognisable in economic terms, by the fact that it is dominated by 'the big three' who employ 100,000 out of Teesside's working population of 180,000[33] in the production of steel, chemicals and marine engineering. Only 3 per cent of the workers living in Teesside move outside to work, and 90 per cent of those working within its boundaries live there.

The basic community of interest is also patent from the number of larger units already operating there; the Tees Port Health Authority, the Tees Valley and Cleveland Water Board, the Tees Conservancy Commission and the Wear and Tees River Board. Other patterns of population movement serve to give the conurbation greater unity; the use of Central Middlesbrough and Stockton market for shops and cinemas; the migration at weekends to football matches, the racecourse, and to the coast at Redcar. The Local Government Commission, which preceded the Maud Commission, said in 1959: 'For these reasons we find it an inescapable conclusion that Teesside is now a single economic, physical and social entity, in which, despite the inadequacy of its bridges, the Tees has served as an industrial stimulus and unifying force for the whole area.'[34]

Factors relating to demand for recreation
It is clear that the Northern Region, despite industrial diversification since the 1930s, has been further deprived of high income earners even since 1961. This does indicate that the North East and Teesside may have moved further away, in economic terms, from the centres of affluence in Britain, and the resulting social imbalances are shown in car-ownership patterns, demand for cheaper forms of entertainment and recreation, and in a conservative attitude to changes in the fashion of certain leisure activities. Teesside's employed population is even more highly concentrated in the manufacturing sector than the rest of the North, or North East, and it also has a lower percentage in the service industries. In the urban core Eston, Thornaby and Middlesbrough, which are the main manufacturing towns, show extremely high deviations from the national mean for almost all socio-economic groups, and since these groups are assumed to be identifiable by their common social, cultural and recreational standards and behaviour,[35] then we must also assume a strong deviation, in Teesside's demand for leisure facilities, from that of the nation generally. This means that less money is spent by the less affluent in their leisure time.

The factors of age, life-cycle and extent to which people are educated also determine the quantity and quality of recreational activity taking place within the conurbation. Since Teesside has a much younger population than the national average the high-energy output activities tend to be prominent in any analysis of patterns of expressed demand, and later in the level of provision. It is perhaps for this reason that since 1963, when local authority expenditure on leisure facilities has risen, it is amenities for sport that have received priority treatment, at the expense of those for the arts. To some extent socio-economic groupings correspond to stages in a life cycle, but Teesside's population would seem to be less mobile, socially, so that the central areas are working class, and the commuter villages middle and upper middle class.

Patterns of activity when related to socio-economic groups in Teesside result in three different types of leisure provision. The first is the most unpredictable and must be associated with changes in the socio-economic structure of the population, in that the participation rates will increase rapidly if income levels rise, e.g. golf, squash, sailing and dining out. To a great extent these facilities will be the concern of private investors. Then there are those activities for which demand is relatively constant throughout the life cycle, and where demand is therefore predictable; examples of this type would be social clubs, fishing, walking, indoor sports and artistic events, reading, sightseeing, driving, etc. Provision for these can be and in most cases should be met by the public purse.

And finally there are those activities for which demand in Teesside is relatively low at present, and predictably so, now and in the near future. These include pony trekking, archery, go-karting, winter sports, climbing, opera and ballet, all of which involve high consumer costs and the kind of climatic or social conditions which are not operating amongst the greater part of the population living in the urban core. There are small pockets of affluence in the more remote areas of North Yorkshire, and Shakespeare has been produced outdoors in the grounds of Ormesby Hall, but this kind of private patronage is the exception which proves the rule on Teesside.

Despite increasing mobility and affluence, it is the moderate and low cost activities which will continue to dominate the demand for leisure in the urban core until the end of this century.

It is estimated that the proportion of the Northern Region's population in the top four socio-economic strata will increase by only 0·3 per cent[36] between 1966 and 1980, which is hardly likely substantially to affect demand for high-cost facilities in the area. On the other hand, the Teesside Survey and Plan predicts that car ownership levels will have considerably improved by that date, changing from 12·7 private vehicles per 100 persons in 1966 to 36

vehicles per 100 persons in 1991. This change will apply particularly
to those living in the central areas where family incomes are still
very low and car ownership less than a third of the national figure.

This will increase the effective time/distance range of intra-
urban central places for leisure, in that the river will become less of a
barrier, urban dwellers will move more often inside the conurbation, and will be able to drive further outside of it using the time
previously taken travelling by public transport in recreational
activity. 'It is likely that the weekday average number of person trips
made in Teesside will have more than doubled by 1991. This is
because the number of trips that are made from home to destinations
other than work increases rapidly as car ownership rises. These
mainly include trips made for shopping and leisure.'[37]

With greater personal mobility the population of Teesside may
turn its attention more towards the regional rather than the local
facility, which would give North Middlesbrough and the new Civic
Centre developments there more centrality, and a wider range of
functions than it has had so far. As Professor House sees it 'the
differential development and the continuance of independent urban
traditions have militated against strong centralisation of functions
in Middlesbrough and, given the economic and social dividing line
the lower Tees continues to represent, pose a subtle problem to those
wishing to integrate the conurbation into a more coherent structure'.[38]

From this short study of intra-urban provision it is clear that
recreation can be regarded as a service, or even a good, in the same
way as other commodities. More detailed studies of urban leisure
provision at national, regional and local levels are obviously
necessary. If these are made available the resources of geographers
and planners may be put to better use in applying their analytical
theories to assess and redress the current imbalances in the hierarchy
of urban recreational provision in Great Britain.

1. Countryside Commission Research Registers, 1–3, 1968–70, London;
   Patmore, J. A., 1970. *Land and Leisure*, notes on ch. 1. London.
2. Thubron, I. M., 1970. *Changing provision for recreation and the arts in urban
   Teesside*. Unpublished M.Litt. thesis, University of Newcastle-upon-Tyne;
   Government Social Survey, 1968. *Leisure and planning*, London.
3. Unpublished report on recreation in Teesside. Daily proportion is the average
   of a 7-day week between October 1965 and September 1966, with a 1·5%
   sample of almost ½ million population. The categories of recreational
   activity are defined as follows: outdoor active—all forms of outdoor sport;
   passive—driving, walking, all spectator sports; indoor active—billiards and
   other forms of indoor sport, dancing; cultural—cinemas, theatres, music etc.

4. Outdoor Recreation Resources Review Commission, 1962. *Outdoor Recreation in America*, Washington.
5. Gore, C., and Jackson, R. T., 1967. *Oxford allotments. A tentative study.* Mimeo, Oxford School of Geography. Oxford.
6. *A report on opera and ballet in the United Kingdom, 1966–1969*, 1969. Arts Council of Great Britain. London.
7. Baumol, W. J., and Bowen, W. G., 1968. *The Performing arts. An economic dilemma.* Cambridge, Mass.
8. Arts Council of Great Britain, 1968. *Annual report 1967–8.*
9. University of Birmingham, Department of Physical Education, 1956. *Britain in the world of sport.*
10. Arts Council of Great Britain, 1961. *Annual Report 1960–1.*
11. *Housing the arts in Great Britain*, 1959. London.
12. Arts Council of Great Britain, 1962. *Annual Report 1961–2.*
13. North East Arts Association, 1961. *1st Annual report.* Newcastle-upon-Tyne.
14. *Public patronage and the arts*, 1967. PEP, London.
15. General Register Office. *Census 1961.* Occupation Tables for England and Wales.
16. Coates, B. E., and Rawstron, E. M., 1966. Regional variations in incomes, *Westminster Bank Review*, February.
17. Coates, B. E., and Rawstron, E. M., 1967. Regional incomes and planning, 1964–5, *Geography*, 52, pp. 393–402.
18. Smailes, A. E., 1944. The urban hierarchy in England and Wales, *Geography*, 29, pp. 41–51; Smith, R. D. P., 1968. The Changing Urban Hierarchy, *Regional Studies*, vol. 2, pp. 1–19.
19. The highest value good is that which has the greatest range, that is for which people will travel the greatest distance. Such a good defines the first order of central places. For the simplest exposition see Berry, B. L., 1967. *Geography of Market Centres and Retail Distribution.* Englewood Cliffs, N.J.
20. BTA/University of Keele, 1966. Pilot Recreation Survey.
21. Smailes. op. cit.
22. GRO. *Census 1966.* Migration tables.
23. Arts Council, 1969. op. cit.
24. ibid. Appendix E.
25. ibid. p. 15.
26. Duncan. op. cit.; Southern Sports Council, 1970. *Provision of Major Sports facilities. A standard assessment of requirements.* Reading.
27. For breakdown of theatre types see Duncan. op. cit., p. 94.
28. Burton, T. L., and Wibberley, G. P., 1965. *Outdoor recreation in the British countryside.* Wye College, London.
29. *Teesside Survey and plan*, 1968.
30. Pinches, J. W., 1969. *Report of the department of arts and recreation to the Teesside County Borough.*
31. Senior, D. (Ed.), 1969. *The regional city.* London.
32. ibid.
33. *Report and proposals for the North Eastern general review area*, 1963. Local Government Commission report no. 6.
34. ibid.
35. General Register Office. *Census 1961.* Occupation tables.
36. *Teesside Survey and plan.* 1968.
37. ibid.
38. House, J. W., 1969. *The North East. An industrial geography.* London.

CONCLUSION

The thesis of this book has been that so long as we can isolate certain times as being given over to leisure and certain resources to recreation, then the distribution of these resources and the movements that take place during leisure time should be susceptible to geographical analysis. While leisure and recreation are the concern also of the behavioural sciences, geographers can make their own contribution to the understanding of and the planning for the recreational needs of the population. Such terms as Stockholm's 'summer metropolis'[1] as a particular form of urban region show a recognition of the ability to fit geographical theories, models and concepts into the framework of leisure activity and gain a new perspective of that activity. From another point of view, the comments of those involved in leisure provision as a business show an understanding of changing spatial requirements: 'The resorts around our shores cannot expand fundamentally without a major upheaval which could take years. Let us look to the interior, therefore, for the new tourist development areas [sic].'[2] 'This understanding of changing needs by those who will be responsible for much of the future distribution of a major part of Britain's tourist industry presupposes assistance and advice from those whose interest is in the land and its use and misuse.

Some of the specific methods that geography may bring to a better understanding of movement and distribution of recreational activity have been discussed in preceding chapters. Models of innovation and diffusion of ideas and of fashions may aid the understanding of how areas develop tourist industries and offer the possibility of predicting the future movement of the leisure frontier. Up to the present, the movement of this frontier ever-outward to areas inaccessible to all but a few, subsequently becoming the resort of many, may seem to reverse the usual concepts of marginality and centrality. In recreational terms a marginal position relative to major concentrations of population is often a positive advantage in an age when industrial and commercial pursuits are increasingly centralised. Recreation is one of the few activities that require land on an extensive scale and where concentration is frequently a disadvantage. This form of land-use and its limiting factors are of obvious concern to the geographer.

Other forms of leisure, sports and the arts for example, have locational requirements differing from those of the annual vacation. Analytical methods which the geographer may use to assess the provision for those demands have been suggested in the use of techniques of locational analysis of public provision of selected activities in Britain. Increasingly detailed statistics are becoming available and we may hope for more accurate analyses of particular recreational problems than we are able to offer in this general introduction.

Whilst the use of hierarchy techniques for the study of urban amenity provision seems to be most desirable, the use of network analysis seems most appropriate in the elucidation of patterns of rural, car-based recreation. Where, if anywhere, should amenities be provided if they are to give maximum benefit? What links should be added to or subtracted from the present rural road network?

Of considerable interest to the geographer is the impact of tourism or recreation upon regional economies and ways of life. As can be seen from the bibliographies in this book, far more work has been completed on the continent, especially by French geographers, on this subject than here in Britain. In many ways, the most important impact made on rural areas in wealthy countries by urbanisation and industrialisation has been that of—not factory farms or the loss of rural land but—the demands made by city-dwellers for recreational space. What has been, and what will be the effect of the influx of these people either as day-trippers or weekend residents on rural communities, on land use, on traditional economies? There are many organised pressure groups in Britain who have done much to prevent the destruction of the countryside by industrial and urban forces. However, the rural society which has been responsible for the creation and upkeep of much of our landscape has long undergone a more insidious transformation. The regional geographer will always ask what the effects will be on the region as a whole of such a transformation of society. We have used regional case studies in this book as a simple method of illustrating general points. There is considerable scope for the further study of individual areas for their own sake in this most important respect.

Although we have emphasised the geographical aspects of the subject, geographers are dependent upon other social sciences for answers to questions on both the general nature of leisure and of many of the variables that lead to changes in its expression. Indeed, many of these variables are indirectly being changed daily by national political decisions. Such variables as incomes, working hours, educational facilities, family size, and taste are all generally assumed to be closely related to levels of recreational activity. One would like to see closer studies of these variables and more precise definition of their relationship to leisure.

There appear to be two broad categories of resources available for leisure use. Natural resources are limited in extent and for all of them there must come a time—for some of them that time has arrived—when their use will necessarily be restricted. These restrictions can be achieved by monetary or other forms of discrimination. Such methods would seem to many to be undesirable. It may be possible, however, by use of the second category of resources —man made or man modified—to divert pressures away from such natural resources. However, this latter type of resources is increasingly dependent on public funds for its creation. In view of both these aspects of leisure resources we believe that increasing state intervention in leisure provision is both inevitable and desirable. In the past limited intervention of this kind has at times been unfortunately, if indirectly, far from democratic in its final effects. If in future it is to be more successful then the nature of leisure and recreation must be better known to everyone, not least to geographers.

1. Blumenfeld, H., 1964. The urban pattern, *Ann. Amer. Acad. Pol. & Soc. Sci.*, CCCLII, pp. 74–83.
2. Butlin, R. Reported in *The Guardian*, 18 May 1971.

INDEX